BUILT

THE 5 FOUNDATIONS OF DISCIPLESHIP THAT WILL MAKE OR BREAK YOU.

Cody Spencer

Built

Copyright © 2020 by Author Cody Spencer.

All rights reserved. No part of this publication may be reproduced, distributed, or transmitted in any form or by any means, including photocopying, recording, or other electronic or mechanical methods, without the prior written permission of the publisher, except in the case of brief quotations embodied in critical reviews and certain other noncommercial uses permitted by copyright law. For permission requests, write to the publisher, addressed "Attention: Permissions Coordinator," at the address below.

ISBN: 9798666255650

For information contact :
PO BOX 189
Horseheads, NY 14845
www.codyrspencer.com

First Edition: July 2020

Bible Version Used:
New King James Version (NKJV)
Amplified Version (AMP)
New Living Translation (NLT)

FOREWORD

As a voice committed to raising and releasing the next wave of influencers on the earth, the impact of discipleship is without measure. This would give us plenty of reason why the Apostle Paul discipled Timothy with these words:

"...**train yourself to be godly.** 8 "Physical training is good, but training for godliness is much better, promising benefits in this life and in the life to come."
1 Timothy 4:7b - 8

We can train, study, & research to do anything, but discipleship is about becoming Christlike. When we take the journey, and implement the tools given, we discover who He is. When we discover who "He is" we also discover who "we are" which leads us to know "who we are called to." The "benefits in this life and in the life to come" is knowing your identity, purpose, and finally receiving a full reward on the other side of eternity. Teachers can give you insight & information, but voices of discipleship impart through the journey of discipleship.

If it hadn't been for the discipleship of men & women in my life I would not be who I am and where I am. I'm grateful for the challenges in my habits, the conversations about priorities over preferences, the encouragement to keep pursuing Him when I sensed nothing, and especially the support from coming under covering of those who had the marriages, lifestyle, & integrity I wanted to produce in my life. Nothing can replace these journey points. I refer back to them often.

In a day when discipleship is thought to be done through podcasts & behind pulpits, this book will build personal ownership for your spiritual pursuit of Him. The message you hold in your hands is meant to bring you into a fresh encounter that's sustained your entire life. Only you have the ability to make that a reality - purse this no matter the cost.

Cody is a walking example of what it means to live a "Built" life from discipleship. With so many trying to give the "how to's" of spiritual formation, it's refreshing to have someone who lives the life beyond the one-liners and surface understanding. I've had the unique opportunity to walk with Cody - speaking into his life, marriage, leadership, & calling. I can honestly say the man & the message are the same.

Discipleship is vital if followers of Jesus are going to walk in strength & significance. As you read through the truth in these pages, I beg you, PLEASE do more than underline your favorite thoughts or highlight what challenges you. The key to unlocking a message like this is practice the truth & live out the focuses. I encourage you to pray over what leaps inside of you, let the revelation comb through your heart, examine your life, and produce the life of Jesus in you. I'll be one of the first to warn you, this book will seep into every part of your life. Get ready!

Chris Estrada - Author, Speaker, & Leader

CONTENTS

Title Page...00

Copyright Page..00

Foreword...00

Contents...00

Introduction...01

Foundation 1..01

Foundation 2..42

Foundation 3..54

Foundation 4..72

Foundation 5..82

About the Author..93

Copyright Page..94

FONTS USED:

Helvetica

INTRODUCTION

The heart behind this book is simple. I want to see you live in everything that Jesus has for you. I have seen so many people "start" and then "walk away" and it is heartbreaking. By laying the right foundation, you will never be one of those who walk away from the life Jesus paid for. I want to see you live a fulfilled life of excellence by loving Jesus and loving others. This is also known as the Great Commandment and Commission. By learning to live these two things out in their fullness, you will never desire to look back at your old life or return to it! By the end of this I believe you will be "built" on some of the same principles that Jesus established in His disciples!

I wrote this book with two intentions. The first is to have a conversation with you. This is not a textbook, but a conversation wrapped around the Bible. Second, this is not a book to sit down and read in a single day. The intention is to read until the end of each section, answer the questions, work through them in your own heart, and then discuss the questions and your thoughts about them with another believer.

I believe all followers of Christ should have someone to mentor them, whether they are 60 years or 60 days into life with Jesus. If you can meet with a believer whom you trust and who is committed to you and will be consistent, this process will be much more effective. Maybe that person is a pastor, church leader, parent, friend or even someone who brought you to church. Share the questions with them, show them your answers and talk through them, commit to follow through and when needed make changes based on these answers, and you will see great growth! Friend, accountability is key to grow and build.

As we go further into this book I don't want the word to scare you; I want it to excite you as you come to know Him as Master, and all that goes along with it! He has never lost or failed; He really is perfect. We tend to follow and be distracted by many things, but fullness of life only comes as we follow one "Master." He who mastered the whole world, and His name is Jesus!

If you are ready to be built by *the* Master craftsman, let's get started!

＃ FOUNDATION ONE

LORDSHIP

* * *

Mark 12:30 "And you shall love the Lord your God with all your heart, with all your soul, with all your mind, and with all your strength.' This *is* the first commandment. 31 And the second, like *it, is* this: 'You shall love your neighbor as yourself.' There is no other commandment greater than these." (NKJV)

Not only do we have a Savior, we have a Lord now, too. And not just any lord, but the Lord of lords, King of kings, the Creator of the universe. We are His and He is ours. We are saved *and* He, the Lord of lords, also desires a personal relationship with us. And, He not only desires a personal relationship with us, He also has a great plan for us! This, in itself is amazing. The Lord of lords has saved us, wants a personal relationship with us, and has a plan for us! But, we need to shift our hearts and minds from simply being saved to the concept of having a Lord in and over our life. This is the most important step in being a disciple! I have seen so many people start their life with Jesus, relieved of sin and saved for eternity, and then, for various reasons, and in different seasons or time, they walk away from it. This is heartbreaking and it is not the plan of God for our lives. In my experience, this most frequently happens because we don't accept and assign Christ the Lordship for which He is due. We do not hear much about this topic, or we may have heard about it but didn't apply the teaching, or we chose to misconstrue it. Lordship is more than just serving Jesus as our Savior; it is giving Him full control and submitting our lives to His plans. (This can sound scary, but it has so many amazing things attached to it.) When we really serve Him as Lord, the full blessing and security He promises is ours. When we don't truly serve Him as our Lord, we can so easily walk away when something or someone is more interesting. We can walk away when someone hurts or offends us, or even when the Bible offends us.We can walk away because we don't want to give something up that we know He wants us to.

We have the choice to serve whatever god we choose in life! Some people serve an attitude, some serve a culture and many even serve a liquid. We choose whom we serve, but it all comes down to three different levels of commitment. Think about it for a second. We have all seen people who appear to be "all-in" with something, and a week later, they stop and never think about it ever again. Or we've seen people who will do something until they get distracted and then flip-flop between the two. Just like so many things that capture our attention in daily life, the same often happens in our relationships with God.

Here are the three levels of commitment to God:

1. Some people serve themselves, kicking God off the throne. Let's call this **Me-Hovah**

BUILT

2. Others serve God part-time, when it is comfortable or when they aren't distracted. We'll call this **Half - Hovah**
3. But the call has always been to give Him all of us! And He is called **Jehovah**.

As we continue, we will discuss more in detail what "Jehovah" means. For now the basic definition we will use is this: Jehovah is one of the formal names for God, the creator and sustainer of everything and everyone in the world.

Question 1: When you hear "Lordship", what is your first response?

_____
_____
_____

Question 2: What primarily controls your life right now? (Emotions, peer pressure, past experiences, God and His Word?)

_____
_____
_____

Question 3: If you were to determine your level of commitment (Me-Hovah, Half-Hovah or Jehovah) what level would your life reflect?

_____
_____
_____

Question 4: Are you meeting with someone to walk and talk through this yet?

_____
_____
_____

Jehovah

There is one true God, and He wants us to love Him and to serve Him because we love Him. At times we get caught up serving Him in a religious or mundane way, but that's certainly not the desire of His heart. Jehovah is His rightful name and place in our heart. Let's talk about the first thing Jesus' teaching *produced* in the heart of His disciples. This topic was Lordship!

We find this interaction in Luke 5:3 "He got into one of the boats, which was Simon's, and asked him to put out a little distance from the shore. And He sat down and began teaching the crowds from the boat. When He had finished speaking, He said to Simon [Peter], 'Put out into the deep water and lower your nets for a catch [of fish].' Simon replied, 'Master...'" (AMP) We aren't told what Jesus taught on that boat, but from one of their first interactions, we see Peter declare Jesus "Master."

Continuing in verse 5, Peter said, "'*Master*, we worked hard all night and caught nothing, but at Your word, I will lower the nets.'" (AMP) We need to see something here: Peter was a professional fisherman. Jesus' trade was not a fisherman; He was a carpenter, Peter was doing all that he knew but it wasn't enough. They had fished ALL NIGHT long - they had to be exhausted. Imagine having a guy show up to your job who doesn't know anything about the industry, and he tries to tell you how to do your job after you've worked an entire shift with zero success. We often end up in this same exact spot when we try to do things on our own and in our own way. Maybe you've said to yourself, "I tried but I'm tired." Could it be that you were fishing without Jesus in your boat?, Without His direction? This is the crossroad of serving Him as Lord. When we

BUILT

are tired and unsuccessful, will we be obedient to His voice in every area and circumstance?

What is the result of following Christ's voice as Master of our lives in every single circumstance? Look at verses six and seven in the same story: "When they had done this, they caught a great number of fish, and their nets were [at the point of] breaking; so they signaled to their partners in the other boat to come and help them. And they came and filled both of the boats [with fish], so that they began to sink." (AMP) Look what happened from that simple step of obedience to Jesus' direction!

- It brought an accelerated result to the work he was struggling with!
- Not just an accelerated result, but a result so abundant that it weighed them down!
- That accelerated result got the attention of their friends so they could see and hear the goodness of God as well!

Peter didn't listen to Jesus' direction because it sounded good or because it made sense. He did it because he had an understanding of Who was giving him direction. We don't know what Jesus said or preached while He was using Peter's boat, but we do know it produced an understanding in his heart that Jesus was the "Master" or the Lord and from that point, Peter would strive to serve Him in that capacity. We see later in their relationship where Peter professes Jesus' Lordship. Take a look at Matthew Chapter 16 starting in verse 16: "Simon Peter answered and said, 'You are the Christ, the Son of the living God.' Jesus answered and said to him, 'Blessed are you, Simon Bar-Jonah, for flesh and blood has not revealed *this* to you, but My Father who is in heaven.'" (NKJV) Here is the truth - when we start to seek God, He will reveal Himself as the "Christ" or as the Master. It is not something we make up or hope for; it is something that is established within our hearts by the Holy Spirit. This is why Jesus died! So that He could reestablish a right relationship with us; to call us from confusion and frustration into a new life with Him as Master!

2 Corinthians 5:17 "Therefore if anyone is in Christ [that is, grafted in, joined to Him by faith in Him as Savior], he is a new creature [reborn and renewed by the Holy Spirit]; the old things [the previous moral and spiritual condition] have passed away. Behold, new things have come [because spiritual awakening brings a new life]." (AMP)

Galatians 2:20 "it is no longer I who lives BUT Christ who lives in me!" (NKJV)

One of the most amazing things happens when we come to Jesus as our Savior. Our sins are removed AND we are made completely new in Him! We don't want to hold onto the "old person" because in God's eyes, that person doesn't even exist anymore. **II Corinthians 5:17** "This means that anyone who belongs to Christ has become a new person. The old life is gone; a new life has begun!" (NLT.) In His eyes, we are brand new, not struggling with old sins and our past, but a 100% new creation. This is so liberating! Many people continue to struggle with who they were and what they did in their past, when it has already been dealt with and settled. I want to encourage you to believe what God said and did and fully walk in this truth - at the moment we believed, we became brand new!

BUILT

Not only are we brand new, but He has now placed Himself inside of us! (John 15:4a "Remain in me, as I remain in you." NLT) This has great significance. Not only are we clean, but we now have surrendered control to He who lives in us. Paul said it like this, "I am an ambassador in chains" (Ephesians 6:20). What he is telling us is that NOW, in Jesus, with Him inside of us, we are representatives of God, ambassadors who are fully empowered to act on His authority, and yet I am in chains. To some, it may be scary, to others contrary to what we've ever learned, but in reality, being in chains to God is the most liberating thing. Being "in chains" to Christ is to live in freedom from the world! Some people choose the chains of alcohol and it destroys their health, finances and family. Some people choose the chains of pornography and it destroys their family and relationships. People live in all kinds of chains of their own choosing.

Before we were in chains to Christ, we had control of our own lives and when we look back, there were some high points, but there were - without question - low points too. When we were in control of our own lives, we were still in chains to our own desires and self-will, which often produced pain, disappointment and a lack of fulfillment. The chains that we are in for Christ are easy to carry. Jesus said it like this, "'For My YOKE is easy to bear and my BURDEN is light,'" (Matthew 11:30 NLT). The yoke is a reference to a piece of wood placed around the neck of an animal to pull farm equipment or a carriage. In effect, it's the device that caused the animals to stay true to the course. What God places on us to stay true to the course and complete our call and purpose in life is easy to bear because it was designed by God to fit us, each, individually and specifically. What the world places on us can never feel natural or light because the world did not create our plan or purpose. The

7

burden Jesus places on us is easy! While the yoke of the world places stress and pain on us, God promises to put an easy burden on our shoulders. We were made and created to be yoked to God and when we choose to live in those "chains" it will be light, easy and produce the blessing of God.

Question 1: What are the old chains that you were set free from?

_____
_____
_____

Question 2: What are the new "chains" you have and what freedoms do they offer?

_____
_____
_____

The Throne

At the center of our hearts is a "throne," and with every day, hour and decision, we determine who sits on this throne. There is always someone or something on this throne; it is never left unoccupied. The greatest and most desirable position is for Jesus to be sitting on the "throne" of ours hearts at all times. This is when He is actually Jehovah or the Lord of our lives! It's my goal, by the time you finish this chapter, to convince you to allow Him to be *your* Lord, every day, every hour and with every decision. Inside of His Lordship is every single thing we are looking for, and every single thing that will bring us to a fullness of satisfaction. Can you imagine a life where you are fully satisfied - all the time? The benefits of having Him as the Lord of our life are endless. When we go to him fully, and abide in, here is a small list of what will be given to you:

You are more than a conqueror. (Romans 8:37)
You are given all authority. (Luke 10:19)
You are anointed by God. (1 John 2:27)
You are part of a holy generation. (1 Peter 2:9)
You have the Holy Spirit. (Acts 1:8)
You have access to a full and overflowing joy. (John 15)
You are complete. (Colossians 2:10)
You live out the good works you were made for. (Ephesians 2:10)
You have access to the fullness of peace. (Philippians 4:6-7)
You are favored. (Psalm 5:12)
You are the salt of the earth. (Matthew 5:13)
You are the light of the world. (Matthew 5:14-16)
You are a son/daughter of the most high God! (Galatians 4:6)

Question: Doesn't it make sense to give Him the throne?

_____

_____

_____

Jesus is Lord

Luke 6:46 "So why do you keep calling me 'Lord, Lord!' when you don't do what I say?" (NKJV)

Lordship is essential for a relationship with God. But what exactly is it? Is it control? Is it slavery? No, Lordship in a relationship is different from Lordship in religion. Lordship in religion is a requirement to fulfill, demanding our output and effort only. The Lordship of a relationship is mutual: "Jesus is the Lord of my life and I serve him. In return, He gives so much back that I want to serve Him more." And so it goes. True relationship with Him means we don't want to disappoint Him by going back and forth, calling Him Lord but not fulfilling all that He asks us to do.

The word "Lord" refers to a "lord or master, a person exercising absolute ownership rights." God's presence in our life is two-fold; He is both our Lord and our Savior. Sadly, many Christians only accept His position as Savior because it holds the benefits of a secure eternity, but they shy away from His position as Lord. His position as Lord of our lives moves us into a position of submission and safety. We do what He asks us to do and we live how He asks us to live.

The Bible shows us that what He did while He was on this earth established Him as Lord! The truth is, He is above all else. He is Lord not only of the good things, but He also has authority over the bad. Check out how Philippians 2 says it, "He humbled Himself in obedience to God and died a criminal's death on a cross. Therefore, God elevated Him to the place of highest honor and gave Him the name above all other names, that at the name of Jesus every knee should bow, in heaven and on earth and under the earth, and every tongue declare that Jesus Christ is Lord, to the glory of God the Father." One day every single knee will bow down and every tongue will declare He is the Lord. I prefer that we do it out of a heart of love, and so does the Lord And in the end, I believe you will too!

In order for Him to truly be Lord of our lives, we need to consciously and consistently determine that He will remain on the throne of our hearts at all times. And, if we slip back onto the throne, we need to have the wisdom to get up and allow Him to be the Lord of our lives again. True story: this is not the easiest thing in the world to do. It's against our human nature to live and act like this. Later, we'll discuss how to make sure this stays in order. But if we do sin, He is faithful and just to forgive us (1 John 1:9). Do not waste your time trying to hide sin or fight with Him. It is a losing battle with Someone who only wants you to win.

Question 1: When it comes to Lordship, do you think your relationship with Jesus is strong enough to give Him full control? What could you do to make it stronger?

_____

_____

_____

Question 2: Is it hard for you to admit to the Lord when you are wrong? What do you do when you first recognize it? What do you think you should do?

_____

_____

_____

Relationship

When we serve Jesus as our Savior, we receive forgiveness and have access to eternity together with Him. Unfortunately, many people stop right there, leaving many unopened promises and plans. Think about it like this: You're 8 years old and it's the morning you've been waiting for all year. You've dreamed of this morning, begged your parents for peeks and hints of what might be coming, and maybe you even bargained with God to speed up the calendar. It's Christmas morning. You wake up to the crisp morning air, the sun hasn't risen yet, but you don't even look at the clock before throwing off the blankets and sprinting downstairs. You run up to the table where you had left cookies and milk the night before and let out a squeal of delight - both are now gone with just a few crumbs in their place! Your eyes dart to the Christmas tree - gifts, gifts everywhere. Without a second thought, you begin to rip them open one by one, wrapping paper flying as you go. Right in the middle of this gift-opening extravaganza, just when things are getting exciting, you feel a warm hand on your shoulder; "Honey, it's only 4:30 a.m., Go back to bed until we are all ready to get up." Your head drops and shoulders slump as you saunter back up the stairs. After a couple of torturous hours, it's finally time to enjoy Christmas morning and the gift opening continues. With just three beautifully wrapped gifts to go - you sit back for a moment and think to yourself; "Hmmm I don't want to open anymore. I am content."

I don't know about you, but this never happened to me! We always want ALL of what's under the tree. Unfortunately, though, when we only come to Jesus as our Savior, that's exactly what we're doing. We're content to only get some of what God has for us, but not *all* of it. There are some interesting reasons for folks to stop at that point. For some, it's fear, for others, it is commitment issues or past hurts that we allow to linger in our hearts. And for a few, it is simply that we don't grasp or aren't taught all that this new life Jesus has for us can bring us. But whatever it is, I want to encourage you to give Jesus all of you. Don't just come to Him as Savior, but as your Lord. If He is not Lord of all, He is not Lord at all!

Let's talk more about the importance of Lordship. Not only does giving Jesus His full lordship give you access to certain things, but often, those who don't take the full step with Jesus eventually walk away from the relationship. My desire with this book is to equip you to walk this relationship out with Jesus as your Lord for the rest of your life. To get there, we have to understand and then implement what our culture considers a scary word: Submission. But, it's not as scary as you think, because submission to His authority actually leads to an authentic relationship. This is always His end goal: a real and genuine relationship with His people. But because he is Lord, the relationship functions on His terms (submission). Allowing His Lordship shows the trust that we have! We can all agree, every relationship needs to have trust!

Submission to God is truly simple: it's saying, "God, I trust you more than I trust myself, more than my feelings or how things seem right now." If we can trust God with our eternity, we can surely trust Him with every other area of our life. If He can keep us out of Hell, surely he can take care of everything else in our lives. Whether it be a deep, personal wound, something we struggle with that's sinful, or even an when He asks us to do something that makes us uncomfortable. He is always working ahead of us for better things than we can ask, think or imagine (Ephesians 3:20). Knowing that He is working to outdo our wildest dreams makes it easy to trust Him in any instance or any circumstance.

Proverbs 3:5-6 says it likes this, "Trust in the Lord with all your heart, and lean not on your own understanding; In all your ways acknowledge Him, and He shall direct your paths." (NKJV)

Isaiah 55:8-9 says this "'My thoughts are nothing like your thoughts," says the Lord. "And my ways are far beyond anything you could imagine. For just as the heavens are higher than the earth, so my ways are higher than your ways and my thoughts higher than your thoughts." (NLT)

With these two truths in mind, it shouldn't be difficult to lay down any reservation and allow Him to be Lord because we can trust Him "on the throne of our heart." God is not like man that He lies (Numbers 23:19), so please do not make God pay for man's mistakes or your current lack of trust in them. How do we do this? Sometimes, we blame God for horrific situations they have been through such as an abusive home life, being abandoned by a father or mother. Instances like this normally cause people to blame God and turn from him in anger. And then we make Him pay for it by keeping our distance from Him (like we are punishing Him!) But, He is not like us. He cannot lie to us! He is not an absent or negligent Father. We can fully trust Him and have a real relationship with Him. This is not about just showing up to church every week (yes, it's important); this is really about having a real and genuine relationship with Jesus Christ!

Our relationship with the Trinity (God, Jesus, Holy Spirit) should work very similarly to how other relationships should work. Good relationships take effort, they don't just happen. And there are always a few things to keep in place for success.

The first is continuous learning. In a relationship, we need to really get to KNOW the other person, and continue to try to learn more about them. The Lord has made that very accessible to us .He has given us the Bible - 66 books that reveal who He is - His nature, His desires for us, and His love for us!

The second is communication. We call this prayer. Prayer is not chanting large words or repeating words over and over. At its very core prayer is simply talking with Jesus from your heart.

BUILT

Having a conversation and giving him the opportunity to talk with you through His Word and the Holy Spirit.

The third is showing honor. We do this through worship and giving. I'm sure you have seen someone sing a love song to a significant other or sacrifice to buy them a great gift. It is literally the same thing. How do you show love? Show it to Jesus.

Jesus wants a real, daily relationship with you! That was His original intention for creating man and that is what I would encourage you to give Him, because that is Jesus at His best! He will never withhold from the relationship; why would He die for us just to ignore us? His will is that no one should live this life without knowing Him (2 Peter 3:9) and having a relationship with Him. I challenge you to make this the relationship you focus on most in life!

Question 1: What is the biggest struggle you have with submission?

_____

_____

_____

Question 2: Do you really believe that you have a better plan than God does? Think about your life when you run it; what mistakes do you think could have been avoided if you had let God run it?

_____

_____

_____

Question 3: Do you have "trust" problems? If yes, are they worth making God pay for them?

_____

_____

_____

Lordship Shows Love

In every relationship, we can expect expectations, whether it's parent to child, boss to employee or even a romantic relationship. The same is true for our relationship with the Lord. Jesus said it like this to His disciples in John 14 verse 15 "If you love Me, keep My commandments." (NKJV) Consider how this happens naturally in your best human relationships. When we recognize and consider all that Jesus has done for us, not only dying on a cross so that we could be free from sin, but what He also did for our bodies to be whole and healthy, and so that we would have "nothing missing, nothing broken and nothing lost" (Bishop Rick Thomas). But wait... there's more! Not only do we have everything in order, but now we can also "approach the throne of God boldly!" Think about it; we can come and stand in front of God like the loving Father that He is because that's what Jesus did for us! When we take inventory of all this, it is easy to have a response of obedience that is driven by love, but If that relationship is simply following rules, it will drift into religion and eventually lead to us walking away.

His intention has always been love! We can go all the way back to Deuteronomy (written thousands of years ago) and see God setting expectations as he spoke to His people about love. Deuteronomy 6:5 says it like this: "You shall love the Lord your God with all your heart, with all your soul, and with all your strength." and Jesus repeated something very similar in Matthew 22:37: "Jesus said to him, 'You shall love the Lord your God with all your heart, with all your soul, and with all your mind. This is *the* first and greatest commandment.'" (NKJV) And, He showed love toward us first. The Bible teaches us that while we were still sinners, Jesus died for us (Romans 5:8), and if that's not love, I don't know what is. All He is

BUILT

asking for is our love in return for His! We tend to "love" a lot of things but have any of those things ever made a sacrifice of love like Jesus did?

Let's explore another aspect of the throne. Merriam-Webster defines the act of bowing to mean "to bend the head, body, or knee in reverence, or submission." For those who have made Jesus their Lord, bowing at the throne is where we belong, and places Him in His rightful place as Jehovah (Lord) of our life! It is a lot like a story Jesus told in Matthew 13:24-30.

"Another parable He put forth to them, saying: 'The kingdom of heaven is like a man who sowed good seed in his field; but while men slept, his enemy came and sowed tares among the wheat and went his way. But when the grain had sprouted and produced a crop, then the tares also appeared. So the servants of the owner came and said to him, "Sir, did you not sow good seed in your field? How then does it have tares?" He said to them, "An enemy has done this." The servants said to him, "Do you want us then to go and gather them up?" But he said, "No, lest while you gather up the tares you also uproot the wheat with them. Let both grow together until the harvest, and at the time of harvest I will say to the reapers, 'First gather together the tares and bind them in bundles to burn them, but gather the wheat into my barn.'" (NKJV)

What is Jesus saying here? Honestly, it's very simple. They knew that in the time of harvest there was one distinguishing mark between the wheat and the tare. The wheat would have fruit (something of value) and the tare would have none. The fruit on the wheat would weigh it down to the place that it would BOW over and the tare would remain standing straight up. What the Lord is looking for is those who are willing to bow in genuine love and not remain standing straight up (walking in their own will). It's a wonderful word picture of submission in our relationship with Him!

I would challenge you to take some time in prayer and worship to ask yourself and the Lord where you currently stand in view of these topics. Does your love for Him equal what He deserves? Is your relationship with Him active and passionate? When these two things are in order, His Lordship is the next natural thing to fall in order!

It is an "every" decision - every day, every moment, every circumstance - to keep Him on the throne. This is something that we consciously and consistently must keep in the forefront of our minds. As in any relationship in life, it must be worked on in order for it to have growth - if you put little to nothing in, you can expect little to nothing back! It can be easy to slip into old patterns (or even develop new behaviors!) that pull us away from serving Jesus as our Lord, if we choose not to take responsibility for our relationship. Proverbs 4:23 tells us to "guard our heart above ALL else because it determines the course of our life," (NKJV) and this is the core truth of loving Jesus. Guard that relationship by making every moment and decision in the context of loving Him and keeping Him as the Lord of your whole life!

Question 1: What is one thing you can do today to "love God more"?

_____
_____
_____

BUILT

Question 2: Would you consider yourself a wheat or a tare? Why do you think that? Consider what you are willing to do to change that.

_____

_____

_____

Me-Hovah

What exactly is the Me-Hovah? It's when we act though as we are the God of our own life.This is the position that Jesus ultimately saved us from. I know this is not fun to hear but it's really why we were in the mess we were in or had the dissatisfaction we did. We were sitting on the throne and doing what pleased us most.It does seem much easier to live life by our feelings and desires, but we all know the outcomes are rarely what we intended or hoped for. Most of us fall into one of two categories when we choose to serve "Me-hovah" instead of Jehovah.

Commitment Issues

We are a "me first" type of culture. That attitude is everywhere! Because of that , we rarely settle down and pour our hearts into anything. We want to be free, doing *what* we want, *when* we want.

Luke 6:46 "So why do you keep calling me 'Lord, Lord', when you don't do what I say?" (NKJV)

Jumping back to the above statement made by Jesus, it becomes more clear to us just how important His lordship really is, as well as our response of radical obedience to that lordship. In fact, He explains that our response of obedience is more than important, it's essential if our desire is to live a stable life, unmoved by circumstances, but instead, always standing firm. Read the following line a few times over: As Hudson Taylor said, "Christ is either Lord of all, or He is not Lord at all."

And here is the heart of the matter: Becoming a disciple of Jesus Christ requires total self-denial. It is all about Him. This is a powerful challenge! Jesus said it in Luke 14:33 "So you cannot become my disciple without giving up everything you own." (NLT) A common theme in the Scripture is Jesus "testing" the hearts of people to see where their commitment really was. I mean, NO ONE likes to share somebody that they are in a relationship with! That is certainly true of God. He said it like this in Exodus 20 verse 3: "You shall have no other gods before Me" (NKJV) Honestly, this is a fair request from the creator of the universe to His creation. And we know from reading about Jehovah that He wants to add things into your life, not take things away. God wants to know that what He has placed in our hands hasn't taken control of our hearts. That we will be obedient with what He has trusted us with and not let it become more important to us than the giver.

Question 1: Do you have commitment issues? Why? What are they?

_____

_____

_____

Question 2: If yes, are they worth keeping?

_____

_____

_____

Selfishness

We all know someone who uses people to get the things they want. Maybe it's even happened to you. You thought that you had a great relationship, but later you found out that the person's only interest is what you could offer to them. It's a horrible feeling; especially when you were committed and gave everything that you had to the relationship. While it is sad, hurtful and wrong, people do this to the Lord all of the time. They look at this relationship more in terms of "what can I get?" instead of "what can I give and look Who I get?" This isn't a new problem. In fact, it's easy to see why some people live like this. When it comes to serving the Lord, it's a great option to escape hell and have some amazing benefits offered to you, but , again, that one-sided "what can I get?"relationship makes it easy to walk away and remove your access from the Lord. Let's look at one young guy from the Bible!

In Luke 18 verses 18 through 23 we find the story of the "Rich Young Ruler." "Now a certain ruler asked Him, saying, 'Good Teacher, what shall I do to inherit eternal life?' So Jesus said to him, 'Why do you call Me good? No one *is* good but One, *that is,* God. You know the commandments: "Do not commit adultery," "Do not murder," "Do not steal," "Do not bear false witness," "Honor your father and your mother."' And he said, 'All these things I have kept from my youth.' So when Jesus heard these things, He said to him, 'You still lack one thing. Sell all that you have and distribute to the poor, and you will have treasure in heaven; and come, follow Me.' But when he heard this, he became very sorrowful, for he was very rich." (NKJV)

When we first read this story it seems as if this young man is asking the right question; a question we have all asked ourselves - "how do I get to heaven?" But when you really look at it, the question in itself is absolutely selfish. He knew what he needed to do; it was not about the rules. He would have known this from his childhood. The Jewish people have a prayer that they quote every night called the "Shema" and part of that prayer is found in Deuteronomy 6 verse 5 and it says: "You shall love the Lord your God with all your heart, with all your soul, and with all your strength." (NKJV) The command was to love God with everything that they had! That young man got it twisted, thinking it was about the *rules* when it was really about *love*. When we love someone, it's a natural desire to fulfill the expectations that they have. The sad part about this story is that the rich young ruler wanted eternity more than he wanted the Father! I pray that your walk never turns into a selfish state of only wanting eternity. I pray that it is and always will be focused around loving God.

Jesus exposed this man's selfishness. It wasn't about the money; it was about his heart. He had something in his heart that he was unwilling to surrender to the Father. His acts of rule-filling service became more important than the intention of the command of God. Anything in our lives (even acts of service!) that comes before God is an idol that must be removed. We can only serve ONE God. If we are serving any other thing, we are actually only serving ourselves. May we never put our desires in front of loving God or His command on our lives!

Question: What is in your heart that you would not surrender to God?

BUILT

Serving God for heaven is still really only serving self. It is motivated by self-preservation, but it will quickly disappear when something else is more interesting. Jesus' disciples lived such an amazing example of how we should live as well. Right after they watched this young man turn away, they had a discussion about who could inherit eternal life, and in verse 28 in the 18th chapter of Luke, Peter makes this statement: "'We have left all we had to follow you!'" (NKJV) If we really want to inherit eternal life, it is never about self. A true disciple will leave everything to follow Jesus! Remember, this is about love. We have all seen love make people do extreme things. *The remedy to selfishness is true love.* Jesus exemplified this and spoke about it in John 15 verse 13: "'Greater love has no one than this, that someone lay down his life for his friends (NKJV).'" He was talking about Himself going to the cross and now He's asking us to lay down our desires, our life, and to go after Him!

The great part about laying down all we have for Jesus is that it always results in Him out-doing us! If we keep reading the interaction in Luke 18, but now in verse 29 and 30, we see the results of serving God out of a heart of love. It says this: "So He said to them, 'Assuredly, I say to you, there is no one who has left house or parents or brothers or wife or children, for the sake of the kingdom of God, who shall not receive many times more in this present time, and in the age to come eternal life (NKJV).'" When we do lay down our life and go after Him, there is a reward that He leaves with us!

Half-Hovah

The silent and sneaky attack to destroy the relationship Jesus has intended for us all is here!

The mistake I have made before - and strive to not continue to make - is a common one that I want to warn you about. This is the mistake of "half-cheeking" the throne to your heart with Jesus. It's sharing the throne with Jesus to protect our own desires, interests and fears. It's sharing the throne that you've claimed to have given to Jehovah. It's serving Him as half-hovah and it is dangerous! When we're scared, nervous or just plain selfish over an issue, it's easiest to take back control. But, will it produce the best outcome for yourself and your relationship with God? Sure it feels good in the moment, but what does it do for our future and our present relationship with God?

All or Nothing

Take a look at this powerful story found all over the internet, originally told by a Haitian pastor: A certain man wanted to sell his house for $2,000. Another man wanted very badly to buy it, but because he was poor, he couldn't afford the full price. After much bargaining, the owner agreed to sell the house for half the original price with just one stipulation: He would retain ownership of one small nail protruding from just over the door. After several years, the original owner wanted the house back, but the new owner was unwilling to sell. So the first owner went out, found the carcass of a dead dog, and hung it from the single nail he still owned. Soon the house became unlivable, and the family was forced to sell the house to the owner of the nail.

BUILT

The Haitian pastor's conclusion: "If we leave the devil with even one small peg in our life, he will return to hang his rotting garbage on it, making it unfit for Christ's habitation."

Oftentimes, people will come to the Lord with certain conditions on what they will keep for themselves. Their attitude is, "God you can have all of me, well actually, you can have most of me, but there are certain things I just can't let you see." These "things" could be anything, from sin, to offense, or simply a refusal to give up simple ideals - the scale is wide.

There is a story in Genesis 35:2 "So Jacob told everyone in his household, 'Get rid of all your pagan idols, purify yourselves, and put on clean clothing. We are now going to Bethel, where I will build an altar to the God who answered my prayers when I was in distress. He has been with me wherever I have gone.' So they gave Jacob all their pagan idols and earrings, and he buried them under the great tree near Shechem." (NLT) The problem is, they were not destroyed. They might have given them up but they still existed. If we are going to be all-in there cannot be anything left to come back for. Don't bury what God has called you to burn!

Many times people become comfortable with sin. We never want to come to a place where we see our sin but aren't actually convicted of it. Conviction is when we become aware of our sin (mistakes) through the Holy Spirit (John 16:8). You know it is conviction when it lines up with the Word of God, it directs you closer to God and it removes distractions from God in your life. We have a choice to make when we become aware of conviction. We can make it right or we can ignore that warning. If we are living in a position of half-hovah, we will only make right what is easy, when it's easy for us, and if we truly want to because we recognize what making it right will do for us. This is a scary thing! Conviction is God's way of saying that our relationship is out of line. When we ignore that warning, we are choosing to keep a clear separation in our life from God. We are literally saying "God, I don't care that I'm hurting our relationship, I'm choosing _____ over you!" As we discussed earlier, He is an ALL-IN kind of God. Exodus 34:14 shows us part of God's nature and heart toward us: "'For you shall worship no other god, for the Lord, whose name is Jealous, is a jealous God.'" (NKJV) I challenge you to embrace conviction. It will ensure that you leave no small peg above your door. When we run from conviction we are actually running straight into the arms of disobedience!

Question 1: What is the "peg" in your life?
_____
_____
_____

Question 2: Are you happy with what that "peg" has been producing?
_____
_____
_____

Question 3: Are you ready to listen to your conviction? Even though it might hurt?

_____
_____
_____

Owner's Closet

Have you ever rented a condo before for a short time, like a vacation, or been with someone who has? In most of these situations, the majority of the space in the condo is yours to enjoy, unless there is an "owner's closet." This closet is filled with some of the owner's personal belongings and is completely off-limits to the renter. This is a strong word picture of what many people do in their hearts with God. So many of us treat God like He's a tenant renting space in the condo of our lives - He can have the majority of the space but there are certain areas He just cannot go near.

Jesus is always calling, but it is up to us whether or not we respond. We qualify or disqualify what we answer to based on our commitment. If a solid foundation has not been laid, it is easy for a person to walk away. Let's think about this by looking at two different examples. Our first example is someone who has been part of the church for a relatively short time. Let's say about 3 months. This person has been a part of God's family, learning and growing, building relationships and even beginning to serve in some capacity. Sounds great right? Yes, BUT, they have done all of this without building the firm foundation of learning about God's crucial role as Lord. This always proves itself before long. Let's say in this scenario, the lust issues that have been pushed down on the inside since coming to Jesus start to come up. Without the firm foundation of Lordship, it is easy to give into temptation. On the flip side, many in the church have been attending for years and have worked out the more simple issues, yet they have a hurt or offense deep within their hearts that they cannot get over or give up, and in turn, after years of investment, they walk away. So really, it doesn't matter whether they have been part of what God is doing for five years or even for as long as fifty. Without this sure foundation of Lordship, they are very prone to leave.

It's often easy to confront the very evident things - but what about those things hidden in the dark places on the inside of us that we don't want anyone to see? It's only when, and because, we place God at the very forefront of our lives that those deeply hidden things within us can be worked out.

Jeremiah 17 verses 9 and 10 say it like this: "'The human heart is the most deceitful of all things, and desperately wicked. Who really knows how bad it is? But I, the Lord, search all hearts and examine secret motives. I give all people their due rewards, according to what their actions deserve.'" (NLT) Let's start with the good news first. The Lord is checking out our hearts and will show us where we may have an "owner's closet." The bad news is, most of us still have an owner's closet that needs to be opened up to Him! However, once He has been given the key to the closet, and you allow him to actually open it, you will be better off in every aspect. If it's sin you've hidden in there, you'll find freedom from giving it up. If it's hurt or offense, you'll find healing. If it's fear, you can be encouraged and find security! We need to allow Him to search us! His Word leaves nothing in the darkness and brings everything to the light. In the books of both 2 Samuel and Psalms, David demonstrated his understanding of the importance of His Word in this area: "'O, Lord, you are my lamp. The Lord lights up my darkness.'" (2 Samuel 22:29 NLT) "Your Word is a lamp to guide my feet and a light for my path." (Psalm 119:105 NLT) There was no question to David, and there should be no question for us, but allow me to ask anyway, if the Word is not the lamp and light for our lives, what is?

Remember, if the idea rings true that you have an "owner's closet", it shows who still has ownership of the house and the throne of your heart!

Question: Do you have an "owner's closet"? What do you keep in there? What keeps you from giving that to Him?

_____
_____
_____

Kingdom Over Culture

"Do not be conformed to the pattern of this world, but be transformed by the renewing of your mind. Then you will be able to test and approve what God's will is - his good, pleasing and perfect will." (Romans 12:2 NKJV)

To "conform" means to follow one's life-long patterns. We know that a lazy life often results in poverty, lying results in a lack of trust, and sin results in death. Our patterns will always determine our results. How do we get different results: by shifting our minds and hearts to the right patterns. Too many people are *disciples* of the culture they are living in or have grown up with and is often the opposite of the culture of God's Kingdom. A simple definition of *disciple* is someone who listens to and follows the teachings of someone else. They are a follower and/or a learner, so a disciple of Jesus will listen to Him, learn from Him and try to live like Him.

Living life as a disciple of culture instead of Jesus is where many of us start,, but in the end, culture does not have the final say., God's Word has the final say. He is the Lord and that will not change, no matter the cultural pressure. Romans 12 is one of the most direct passages about culture. Paul, the author, makes it simple for us: do not comply with the way the world does things. Instead, change *your* ways by learning from God's Word, which remodels (renews) your mind.

The way the world operates may be fun for a moment, but the world's long-term negatives far outweigh any moments of enjoyment. Please know and understand this truth:God's Kingdom is exclusive to those who truly follow His Word. This is not a popular message in the world, but Jesus clearly lets us know in Matthew 7:13-14 "You can enter God's Kingdom only through the narrow gate. The highway to hell is broad, and its gate is wide for the many who choose that way. But the gateway to life is very narrow and the road is difficult, and only a few ever find it." (NLT) That way, His way, while it may be the narrow path, is the only way. Bending to cultural pressures takes you through the wide gate. . His Word is enough and it is good, and it needs to be held above all else, which is truly the narrow way, according to the world's standards.
We can easily fall into 1 of the 2 common mistakes in our walk with

God that we find in Jeremiah 2 verse 13: "For my people have done two evil things: They have abandoned me—the fountain of living water. And they have dug for themselves cracked cisterns that can hold no water at all!" (NLT) First, we forget Jesus and allow other things to take His place. Of course it's never on purpose and it's normally innocent. It looks like this: In the morning, instead of prayer and worship, it's the news. At night, it's no longer devotional time, it's now time for your favorite TV show. Not that any of these things are wrong, but when they take the place and time of Jesus, we have forsaken him. "We have traded joy for entertainment" (Leonard Ravenhill) and attempted to fill the void in our life with other things, forgetting that Jesus is the fountain of living waters (AKA *all* we are looking for). Secondly, we create things (dig cisterns that hold no water) that replace who God is and what He does in our life. Though we work hard at it, we cannot create anything in the natural that quenches, provides or satisfies as God does. The boy/girl, the drink, the like on your post, the

BUILT

acceptance of others, the money, the power - none of it can replace what God can do. It is like a broken vase; it will always have a leak!

If you live like this, in your half-hovah reality, eventually you will slide to one side of the chair. Either all the way on it as your own god once again, or off it to give God His rightful place as Lord. Sadly, many people slide all the way on, because in this struggle we must realize that "If He is not Lord of all, He is not Lord at all," and give over everything to God. It is not worth serving Him with "half of your life" because He cannot accept that! He was speaking to a church in Revelation chapter 3 verses 15-16 and said it like this: "'I know your works, that you are neither cold nor hot. I could wish you were cold or hot. So then, because you are lukewarm, and neither cold nor hot, I will vomit you out of My mouth.'" (NKJV) He was speaking to a church and he was speaking directly to us. Jesus is not looking for half of our lives when He sacrificed ALL of Himself! He wants and deserves everything.

Question 1: In what area of your life do you slide into "half-hovah"?

_____

_____

Question 2: How can you make sure that does not happen in the future? Are there practical steps you can implement?

_____

_____

Question 3: Do you "intend" to give him the whole throne? What do you think are the repercussions for the wasted time until you do?

_____

_____

Keys to Serving Jehovah

We are all searching for a few basic things. For some of us, it's peace; for others it's love, and there's joy or security, and on and on and on. Here is the simple truth, unfathomable to those who don't have a relationship with Jesus - when we give up our search for these things in the world, we can find what we have always been looking for. It sounds crazy but it is the truth, through Jesus, He holds all of it!

Matthew 6:33 "But seek first the kingdom of God and His righteousness, and **all** these things shall be added to you." (NKJV)

It's hard to understand outside of faith. And it sounds too simple, as if it could never really happen. But I have news for you: God cannot lie! And, you know what, It is simple! He has made it simple for us to follow and to live out. Seeking the kingdom of God is much easier than some people make it out to be. Romans 14 verse 17 and 18 give us insight on what this looks like: "for the kingdom of God is not eating and drinking, but righteousness and peace and joy in the Holy Spirit. For he who serves Christ in these things *is* acceptable to God and approved by men." (NKJV) What we need to seek (pursue) is righteousness, peace, and joy in the Holy Spirit! Now all three of these pursuits could have their own books, so we'll only take a glimpse at them.

Righteousness: Is what is right in the eyes of God. When we can seek what is right in His eyes and insist on it, we remain in the "Kingdom."

Peace: Peace of mind, peace with others, peace at heart. It's the ability to take a deep breath with a settled feeling in your mind and heart about what is happening in your current, future and eternal state.

Joy in the Holy Spirit: A supernatural joy that goes beyond your emotions and circumstances. This is not an emotion, but a state of being that is a gift from God; we receive it from Him and can remain in it.

Question: Which of the three (righteousness, peace, or joy in the Holy Spirit) are hardest for you to remain in in your daily walk? What can you do to fight not to lose them?

_____

_____

_____

There is a Fight

"He lives in us and undertakes to transform our nature and our character, our very person and being—so that our spirit and soul, body and blood may become spirit of His Spirit, soul of His soul, flesh of His flesh, bone of His bone, and blood of His blood." (Excerpt From Spiritual Hunger, The God-men and Other Sermons by John G. Lake)

We must realize that there is a fight going on for our spirit. Our flesh and the evil one are not going to go down easily. Jesus transformed us when he saved us, but now we have an enemy that would love to attack that work. If we fight improperly, we can waste a whole lot of time and effort. The fight that goes on in this life is a fight over one of the three parts that make up who you are. We are a spirit, who has a soul, that lives in a body, according to 1 Thessalonians 5:23 (Now may the God of peace make you holy in every way, and may your *whole spirit and soul and body* be kept blameless until our Lord Jesus Christ comes again. NLT) Our *spirit* is what is washed clean, is saved and goes to heaven. The *soul* is made up of our mind, our will and our emotions. And the *body* is simply the thing that houses spirit and the soul while on this earth. This fight is for our washed clean spirit, but if the enemy can infiltrate our soul (mind, will and emotions) we now have a two-on-one fight! The enemy vs our soul!

Your body will always go wherever your soul (your mind, your will and your emotions) goes.The fight is always against our spirit man being the strongest because if the enemy can get your soul (mind, will and emotions) and body to gang up on your spirit, you are in trouble.

Here is the answer to winning the battle against both the enemy and the flesh: "I say then: Walk in the Spirit, and you shall not fulfill the lust of the flesh. For the flesh lusts against the Spirit, and the Spirit against the flesh; and these are contrary to one another so that you do not do the things that you wish." (Galatians 5:16-17 NKJV) Did you notice that the soul was not mentioned? It is because we need to walk in the Spirit! You can get your soul to walk in that same way when you are walking in the Spirit. When we submit ourselves to the Lord, 2 Corinthians 5:17 says that it is our spirit that is washed clean and made new, which means that we have to make an active decision every day to renew our mind (soul).

Consider what David says in Psalm 119:11 "I have hidden your word in my heart, that I might not sin against you." (NLT) To have "hidden" in this case (based on the original Hebrew) something means to treasure it or store it up. The "heart" referred here is the mind, will and emotions of an individual; in other words, our soul. The soul was created by God to be controlled by the Spirit of God, not to independently do whatever it wants, wreaking havoc wherever it goes. Our emotions are not negative, but they are controllable, and are best controlled by being kept in line with God's Word instead of our unpredictable self desires. When we get our spirit and our soul on the same page, every single moment of every single day, the battle is turned to a victory!

Question: Identify when you are in a battle with your flesh. What happens? How can you redirect yourself? How can you "walk in the spirit" every day? Describe what happens when the Spirit has the victory.

_____

_____

_____

Our Advantage

Some people believe that it was likely easier to follow and serve Jesus while He was in human form here on earth, but that is simply not true. He didn't leave us to our own devices! In John chapter 16 verses 5-7 Jesus said: "'But now I go away to Him who sent Me, and none of you asks Me, "Where are You going?" But because I have said these things to you, sorrow has filled your heart. Nevertheless, I tell you the truth. It is to your advantage that I go away; for if I do not go away, the Helper will not come to you; but if I depart, I will send Him to you.'" (NKJV) Imagine being one of His close followers and hearing this? What would you be thinking? Feeling? Saying? "What do you mean, you're leaving? You can't leave us yet! You're sending a helper? Who is He? How can He be to our advantage?" While the questions were understandable, of course, He knew what He was doing. And, of course, He was right!

The Holy Spirit is our advantage. While the disciples had Jesus to teach them and help them grow, they did that without the advantage that we have! Jesus - in the physical sense - was in one place and at one time. The Holy Spirit, is now in each of us who believes. He's inside us! He's leading us, correcting us and empowering us. He is not an "it" or a "thing." Holy Spirit is as much God as God is, and Holy Spirit is His name. He is one-third of the Trinity and available to us at all times, in all places, in every situation.

Advantage Number 1: Holy Spirit is in us!

In the following passages, we can see how this is a biblical truth. In John 14:16-18 Jesus told his disciples: "'And I will pray to the Father, and He will give you another Helper, that He may abide with you forever— the Spirit of truth, whom the world cannot receive because it neither sees Him nor knows Him; but you know Him, for He dwells with you and will be in you. I will not leave you orphans; I will come to you.'" (NKJV) What an amazing promise to His disciples and to us. We are not left to be orphans on this earth. Holy Spirit both dwells in us and with us. This means that every day, in every place, and in every situation, Holy Spirit is with you. We find another promise about Holy Spirit living in us in Romans 8:11. Paul said: "But if the Spirit of Him who raised Jesus from the dead dwells in you, He who raised Christ Jesus from the dead will also give life to your mortal bodies through His Spirit who dwells in you." (NKJV) The giver of life to Jesus' dead body is now dwelling inside of you, giving life to your body! Not only are we *not* orphans, not only do we have Him with us in every moment and in every place, but He is giving our bodies life!

BUILT

Advantage Number 2: He leads us.

For all who are led by the Spirit of God are children of God.
(Romans 8:14 NLT)

When we listen and obey the Holy Spirit, His direction proves that
we are God's children. He is not a God who will lead His children to
destruction and death. He leads us into the promises and plans of
Jesus. In John 14:26 Jesus teaches us that Holy Spirit will teach us
all things and help us remember all things, and in John 16, verses 8
through 13 we see that Holy Spirit will convict the world of sin, and
of righteousness and of judgement and lastly into all truth. When
we listen to our own instruction, we often lead ourselves into trouble
and we make poor decisions. So our second advantage is that we
no longer have to do that, ever. Holy Spirit doesn't get it wrong.
Now, some people teach otherwise about Holy Spirit and His role in
our lives, but the Bible clearly shows us that when we follow the
lead of Holy Spirit, we will know all truth, remember all truth, and be
led into righteousness, judgement and conviction as we need it.

Advantage Number 3: He Empowers us.

Right before Jesus ascended to heaven, His disciples asked Him a
question. His response is noted in Acts 1:8 "'But you shall receive
power when the Holy Spirit has come upon you; and you shall be
witnesses to Me in Jerusalem, and in all Judea and Samaria, and to
the end of the earth.'" (NKJV) The advantage we have here is clear:
we now have access to power! We will get more into this later, but
please know this: You are not weak. You now have the same
amazing power that raised Jesus from the grave living inside of
you, working for you and through you. Whatever God has asked

you to do, you have the strength to do it. The power of God you will receive from Holy Spirit is far beyond any physical or mental limitation.

Holy Spirit, our helper and our advantage, can be in us, leading us and empowering us! Growing in Jesus is not a hard thing, and it's even easier when we live with (abide, give full reign) to Holy Spirit, which is what Jesus wants us to do, because He sent Him to us for that very purpose!

Question: How do I give control over to the Holy Spirit? Keep reading below for details!

What does the Bible say about this? In Acts 19, Paul found followers of Jesus.Trying to understand their spiritual maturity, he asked them if they had been baptized in the Holy Spirit. They responded that they had not even *heard* of the Holy Spirit! Paul's response is in verses 4-6: Paul said, "John's baptism called for repentance from sin. But John himself told the people to believe in the one who would come later, meaning Jesus." (NLT) As soon as they heard this, they were baptized in the name of the Lord Jesus. Then when Paul laid his hands on them, the Holy Spirit came on them, and they spoke in other tongues and prophesied." The baptism of the Holy Spirit is not only for all believers, it's important for all believers. But how do we receive this? You ask for it! The baptism is for all and "tongues" are an indication of the gift (not the gift itself). Here are verses and instances of people receiving this gift.

Acts 2:4 "And everyone present was filled with the Holy Spirit and began speaking in other languages as the Holy Spirit gave them this ability." (NLT)

Acts 10:45–46 "The believers ... who came with Peter were amazed, because the gift of the Holy Spirit had been poured out even on the Gentiles. For they heard them speaking in tongues and extolling God." (AMP)

Acts 19:6 "The Holy Spirit came on them, and they spoke with tongues and prophesied." (NKJV)

Speaking in tongues, wherever mentioned, was not the activity of some but of the whole body of newly Spirit-filled believers. The purpose of the Baptism of the Holy Spirit is not so we can speak in tongues. The reason behind this gift is to give us more power! Remember, the Holy Spirit will lead us and empower us and this is the key indicator of His activation in our lives.

What are some other benefits of this gift? Here is a small list of some of them!

Spiritual encouragement (1 Corinthians 14:4)
Praying in line with God's will (Romans 8:26)
To stimulate our faith (Jude 1:20)
Praying for the unknown (Romans 8:26)
To help us in our weakness (Romans 8:27)
For spiritual refreshing (Isaiah 28:11-12)
To help us control our tongues (James 3:8)

The baptism of the Holy Spirit is a gift, and as a gift, it is free. In Acts 2:39 Peter taught, "'For the promise is to you and to your children, and to all who are afar off, as many as the Lord our God will call.'" (NKJV) We don't need to beg for it, don't need to be saved for 10 years, don't need to jump through certain hoops, or be perfect, we just need to receive. Salvation and the baptism of the Holy Spirit are received in the same way. We must believe it and then receive it through faith and prayer. Now, hearing, speaking or praying in tongues for the first time may be more than a little surprising; this is not at all the same as speaking the English language. To some it sounds like gibberish, but in reality it is a "heavenly language." But, just like hearing French or Spanish for the first time, we don't expect to understand it, but it is completely normal. Once you experience praying in tongues, you will feel its power; but initially, it is definitely different!

Anyone can pray for the Baptism of the Holy Spirit right now with the evidence of speaking in tongues, by praying, this prayer and receiving this gift from Jesus. Just pray this from your heart and believe it in faith: "Father, I thank you for the Baptism of the Holy Spirit in my life. I ask you for this free gift right here and right now. I want to grow in you and be used by you. I also thank you for the gift of speaking in tongues. I believe this is for me and it is a promise from you for all believers. Today, I receive your promise by faith. Amen."

Now, you have this free gift. You may feel some words in your heart to start praying - words that aren't English. Just open your mouth and start to let them roll off your tongue even now. This act of faith releases the evidence of the gift. No, you are not crazy and no you are not making them up.

For more clarification on this, you can ask your local Pastor.

What Now?

This is the first thing that needs to be established in our walk with Him - His Lordship and our willingness to allow Him to be the Lord of our life! When we have fully given Him the throne, we have guaranteed our lifelong relationship with Him. This is just the beginning of what He has for us. This truth needs to be held at the core of our relationship. Some people will "get it" and then over time slip off into serving one of the other "gods." Therefore, we must be sure to remind ourselves daily of our commitment to His Lordship. We do not just serve a Savior; we serve the Lord, the Lord of all! These concepts and verses help us understand His Lordship so that Jesus can reveal Himself to us! Those who develop this "revelation" or "understanding," will not be like those who walk away because we are rooted in the direction of Jesus. Whatever the distraction or issue, it will never be able to change the fact that Jesus is the Lord of your life. May you know this in your heart and apply it to every decision in your life because of the Love you have for Him!

Once you have established Lordship, the order of the next three are less important than the fact that they are established in your heart. The following three chapters are all vital and important - they must be discovered, worked on and implemented into your life! REMEMBER discipleship is not a cookie-cutter process.

Cody Spencer

FOUNDATION TWO

PURPOSE

* * *

Part of following God is recognizing that you have a purpose in this life! There is so much more to life in Christ Jesus than eating, sleeping, having kids and retiring nicely at the age of 65. You have been designed intricately by God with a very specific plan and purpose in mind. When you surrendered your life to Jesus and started this relationship it was not only for you to go to heaven but it was also to get heaven into you, so it could then flow out of you! We have all been given gifts to impact the world. Some or more evident than others, but one thing stands and that is that they are all honorable and acceptable before God because every one of us is made in His image with His great plan in mind. God is a very intentional God. Nothing He has ever created or done was by accident. From the beginning of the earth to every creature that so uniquely walks upon it, God designed each with purpose and intent, and the same goes for us. Inside of being His disciple is finding and following it!

Breathe, life and purpose

Some people believe they have nothing to offer this world, that because of their situation, upbringing or even what that have been told from a young age that they are in a sense "worthless". I believe this is an absolute lie! Do this with me really fast… actually do it!

Take a deep, deep breathe, fill your lungs completely with air. Now let it out slowly and controlled.

An important part of following God is recognizing that you have a purpose in this life. There is so much more to life in Christ Jesus than eating, sleeping, having kids, and retiring nicely at the age of 65. You have been intricately designed by God with a very specific plan and purpose in mind. When you surrendered your life to Jesus and started this relationship, it was not only so you to go to heaven, but it was also to get heaven *into* you so it could then flow *out of* you! We have all been given gifts to impact the world. Some are more evident than others and they are all honorable and acceptable before God. God is a very intentional God. Not one thing He has ever created or done was by accident. From the beginning of the earth to the creation of every being that so uniquely walks upon it, God designed each with purpose and intent, and the same goes for us. Being His disciple means finding and following our purpose!

Success or Satisfaction

We have a choice to make in life. Various kinds of success are available to us, but the only way to have true and fulfilling success and satisfaction is to follow the plan that Jesus has for you. We see millionaires, celebrities, and politicians who all have great apparent success, but for some reason, many live in misery, depression, and in some instances, that despair escalates into them taking their own lives. This can happen for a multitude of reasons but I want to focus on one truth here: **Success does not always guarantee satisfaction** *unless* you are living out God's plan and purpose for your life. You may have recognition in a field of work, you may have a large bank account or you may be able to influence millions of people, but unless you are living in God's plan and purpose for your life, you will never have true satisfaction with those things.

We find a man named Peter in the Bible who was one of the first men to answer Jesus' call to "follow me" (we will explore that next). He was a successful fisherman, owned multiple boats, and even had employees under him. Yet He walked away from all those things when Jesus called him. And yet, we never see him regret it, not even once. What we do see is that after Jesus is crucified on the cross, Peter did return to fishing.

He had stepped back from satisfaction in an attempt to return to where he used to have "success". You will never have satisfaction outside of serving Jesus' call on your life. Peter knew that Jesus had called him to "go and create disciples" but instead, he went back to fishing! Success will never be enough until you can rest your head at night in genuine satisfaction. The only way to access real success and satisfaction is to follow God's perfect plan for your life.

Question 1: What kind of a "success" lures you, that if you let it, it could rob your satisfaction from Heaven?

_____
_____
_____

Question 2: Have you sought God's plan and purpose for your life yet? Has He responded?

_____
_____
_____

If you have not yet, in the next few chapters we will talk about it!

Follow Me

Remember, every single person on this earth has a purpose from heaven. This is how Jesus called His disciples to their purpose: "And Jesus, walking by the Sea of Galilee, saw two brothers, Simon called Peter, and Andrew his brother, casting a net into the sea; for they were fishermen. Then He said to them, 'Follow Me, and I will make you fishers of men.' They immediately left *their* nets and followed Him." (Matthew 4:18-20 NKJV)

It all started with the simplest of commands, but it is the very command that would shape the world. These men were just casually going about their day-to-day business, catching fish to sell, when the call came to follow Jesus. This call went out to them, and also to 10 other men, all from different walks of life, jobs, and backgrounds. The words "follow me" were not dependent on where they had come from or even on their qualifications, but on where they were going. They had no idea where this decision would bring them, but His words were strong enough to influence these men to abandon everything. Becoming a disciple of Jesus is not just for a Sunday service or weekly class, but it's a daily lifestyle of pursuing Him (Luke 9:23).

Question: Will you follow Jesus anywhere He calls you to go?

_____

_____

_____

I Will Make You

Jesus gave them a promise that speaks of forming or creating. And who better than the Creator Himself to make something of us and our lives? We often discount God based upon our personal experiences instead of what He has promised us, His promise is one of purpose and potential, but nothing you or I have encountered in the past can prevent him from fulfilling His promise.

There is no "flaw" that has been overcome that could override the promise of God to make us into fisher of men! People in the Bible often gave God reasons as to why they would not be able to do what He had called them to do. Moses, for instance. God had called Him to go back to Egypt and ask for Pharaoh to let God's people go. Moses responded to God by arguing that his stutter made him less than an ideal candidate for the job. Guess who won that disagreement? See the whole story beginning in Exodus chapter 4. It might not be apparent right now, but God will utilize every piece of each one of us to fulfill what He has called us to do. If you're an introvert, He will give you boldness! If you stutter, and He calls you to leadership, He will make a way. You may not think you have "the right stuff," but God created and planned you for success! God will use those who may appear to be "unqualified" in their own eyes, into something special and specific. This happens over time. Time spent with Him, shaping and molding, and time spent serving with mature believers will start to "make you into" what He created you to be!

Question 1: Will you commit, for the rest of your life, to allow God to "make you" into what He created you to be? Describe specifically what that commitment looks like to you.

_____
_____
_____

Question 2: What do you envision will be your biggest obstacle in doing this?

_____
_____
_____

Fishers of Men

First, the disciples were called: "Come, follow Me." Then they were told that Jesus had a plan for them "I will make you", and then, in the last portion of the verse, they are presented with the preeminent goal - the purpose: "fishers of men."

This call has been extended to each of us. Whoever and wherever you are, if you follow Jesus, this request has been made of you (first, in Matthew 28:18-20 "All authority in heaven and on earth has been given to me. Go therefore and make disciples of all nations, baptizing them in the name of the Father and of the Son and of the Holy Spirit, teaching them to observe all that I have commanded you. And behold, I am with you always, to the end of the age." (NKJV) And in John 3:16, he again demonstrates that it is for all people to be given the opportunity to come to know and follow Jesus. "For God so loved the world, that he gave his only Son, that whoever believes in him should not perish but have eternal life." (NKJV) Show people how to love Jesus. Show people that they truly will not go to Heaven without Him. That is our ultimate purpose in life. We have all been given unique gifts from God, and each gift, talent, or passion is geared from heaven to assist us to win and disciple souls. We want to remember though, not to get so caught up in the "work" of our gift, talent or passion, that we forget the true purpose behind that work, the "what" is to win and disciple souls. If you're a plumber, you're not a plumber who goes to church; you're a Christian who does plumbing!

Ah, but...there is a battle for your purpose, and the enemy will often attack your identity. If he can distract us from our confident knowledge of who we are in Christ, the call and purpose can be forgotten, and he gets the victory. This is why it's vital to keep our sense of identity in order. Remembering that we are first believers in Christ, in front of our nationality, our culture, or our profession, keeps us grounded. We need to not get so distracted with life, work, and church that we forget why we're here - to share the good news of Jesus and bring people into a relationship with Him! This is our first and most important thing in life because it is God's greatest desire! It's so important that we'll spend time talking more about it in the last chapter.

Question: How have you prioritized your profession or lifestyle or culture or even your service to the church above your purpose of sharing the Gospel with others in your life? What can you do to refocus?

_____

_____

_____

Living Life on Purpose

Too many times, we are reactionary rather than purposeful. When we are reactionary, we don't have forward progress because we are too busy reacting!. Too many Christians play defense in order to figure out their purpose and what God has called us to do. We have to switch sides; we have to go on the offense.

One way we are reactionary is to say "yes" to every request that's made of us. If that' s you, then you may need to stop saying yes to everything! When we say yes to everything, we end up being too busy for the one thing we have been called to do. Jesus lived life on purpose and we see it evident in Scripture: "Then Jesus answered and said to them, Most assuredly, I say to you, the Son can do nothing of Himself, but what He sees the Father do; for whatever He does, the Son also does in like manner." (John 5:19 NKJV)

Jesus, the Son of God, only did what He saw God, His Father, do. He was deliberate and on purpose. He was *intentional* about fulfilling the purpose of God in His life. We can live life on purpose and there are two keys that open doors to being purposeful First if you hear God tell you to do it, do it. Second, if the devil tries to distract you, do it even more!

BUILT

David Oyedepo, a powerful man of God from Lagos, Nigeria says it like this: "If God can't take me there, may I never go. If God can't give it to me, may I never have it. If God can't do it, let it remain undone."

Whatever He has called and gifted you to do, stay focused! 2 Timothy 2:4 tells us this "No one engaged in warfare entangles himself with the affairs of *this* life, that he may please him who enlisted him as a soldier." (NKJV) Remove the distractions and fulfill what God has asked you to do. For some, it's running a successful business so they can give to God's work. For others, it is working a role in a company that positions you to share Jesus with them all. And He has called some to work full-time in the ministry. No one is "better than" another. The only real way to succeed is to do what YOU have been called to do and to do it intentionally!

Question 1: What is your largest distraction of doing what God called you to do?

_____

_____

_____

Question 2: How can you remove that distraction?

_____

_____

_____

Question 3: Have you heard God tell you what to do in this life?

_____

_____

_____

If not, pray, ask, and write! The last chapter of this will also help clarify.

Answer the Call

"Marco…" I bet right now in your head you just responded with "Polo!" That's because since we were young, we have been taught that a call is always followed by some type of answer. Our answer to God's call is what matters.

"Then the Lord asked Moses, 'Who makes a person's mouth? Who decides whether people speak or do not speak, hear or do not hear, see, or do not see? Is it not I, the Lord? Now go! I will be with you as you speak, and I will instruct you in what to say.' But Moses again pleaded, 'Lord, please! Send anyone else.' Then the Lord became angry with Moses. 'All right,' he said. 'What about your brother, Aaron the Levite? I know he speaks well. And look! He is on his way to meet you now. He will be delighted to see you." (Exodus 4:11-14 NLT)

Like Moses, we can allow fear and self-doubt to outweigh faith. When we do this, though, we fail to recognize one powerful fact: Indeed, without God, we could not But *with God*, we are more than able!

What if God never provided Aaron? Think how many people have been left in their sin because you didn't speak up? Where would *you* still be if someone never spoke up to you? Believe it or not, SO MANY people are stuck in this position. You may look foolish to the world, it's true. But that doesn't mean you will be unsuccessful. You are an ambassador for the Kingdom of heaven who has been given an assignment. It may appear foolish to some, and you may be planting seeds for others to harvest. But, His Word will not fail to do what it sets out to do, so you can speak in full confidence, representing your King and Lord.

There is a connection between understanding who God is and what He requires of us. Many people think that they understand Him, but then fail to follow Him. It is important that we know about things, but it is equally important that we act on them, too. The difference between knowing and understanding is this - knowing is simply head knowledge. Understanding is applying that head knowledge in everyday living. When He calls you, your response can change the world. No one in the Bible knew the magnitude of their *yes*, yet here we are, still talking about it today!

Question 1: Is there a time you regret saying "yes" to God? Think of a time you said "no" to God. Compare the results.

_____

_____

_____

Question 2: What is one thing you can do to never say 'no' to Him again?

_____

_____

_____

How to Discover God's Intended Purpose For You

I believe you can start living on purpose and in your purpose right now! You start by asking God for direction. His desire is for you to do what He designed you for, so why would He keep it a secret? You may not see the entire picture and that is truly okay! Whatever He asks you to do next will lead into His full plan and purpose. As you become more mindful and obedient to his leading, he will reveal more.

But, while you're waiting, here are a few questions that will help point you in the right direction as well!

Question 1: What are you naturally good at? God made you, therefore, what you are good at and gifted for has come from God Himself. If you can sing, it is a gift from God that should be used. If you can structure an organization in your sleep, you should use it for God! Every gift that you have is at its best when it's used to glorify Him. Remember that it might not look exactly how you thought it might look, but it is definitely part of your purpose. List those talents and gifts that you already have.

_____
_____

Question 2: What moves your heart? Yes, God will use you in areas that you're not 1,000,000% comfortable in at times. But largely, that which moves your heart with compassion or agitation is oftentimes tied to your purpose. (See Nehemiah Chapter 1, Esther, Jonah) List those things that move you.

_____
_____

Question 3: What can you do right now? Maybe you cannot preach to an entire stadium right now, but you have a passion to preach to a small group. Do it. Maybe you are not in a position to do everything you feel called to do yet, but you can start serving and doing something. One of the worst things to do is to wait for the fullness of your purpose but never take steps in the direction of it. List those things that you can think of to do right now, even if they might make you a little uncomfortable.

_____
_____

Example: Maybe you can sing and you're passionate about teenagers finding hope in Jesus. It just so happens your church has a youth group. Go see if they need help with the youth worship team.

BUILT

Example: You have amazing administration skills and you are passionate about the homeless in your community. Go to your local church and see how your skills can be used to help!

What are your next steps? Pray about what you feel you can do and ask God if that is your next step. If you feel Him saying "yes," that is the step to take. If you do not feel a yes, keep praying and asking for direction.

FOUNDATION THREE

LEARNING

* * *

Directly following the call, Jesus began teaching and preaching the good news (Matthew 5-7). While He was spreading the Word, He traveled with his newly recruited disciples. After He called them, He trained them. He knew that in order to develop His disciples into what He needed, He would have to teach them. Jesus doesn't desire us to be ignorant or lacking. His desires are for us to know Him, and know Him in such a way that we become more than just acquaintances, but have a rich, strong relationship. As disciples of Jesus, in order to know what we're supposed to do for Him - know His promises to us, know who we are in His eyes, and be able to stand strong - we need to be taught and educated. This particular step in discipleship is one that will never be "checked off" or fully achieved. An amazing fact of God and the Bible: We can study and search the things of God our entire life and still find new things and fresh impartation each time. But, some preparation is required - we must lay a solid foundation for a lifetime of successfully following Jesus. In the coming sections, we'll look at why this is important, what to learn, and how to use what we learn.

Why Should We Know?

The things of God are discovered in two ways. One is through knowledge and the other is via experience. Both are needed to have a full understanding. If we only text back and forth with someone, but never actually meet, we may know some things about the other person, but we will not be able to fully grasp their personality or intentions. On the flip side, if we only ever see each other casually, but never actually talk deeply and share things, we will only interact on a shallow level. When we learn about God through His Word and also by experiencing Him, it takes us to the next level in our relationship. One of His greatest goals for us (Mark 12:30) is to have us love Him and have a genuine relationship with Him. Growing in our knowledge of God allows us to grow into a deeper relationship with Him and helps us learn to trust His intentions for us.

Reading the Word is how we grow in knowledge. In John 8 verse 31-32, Jesus said it like this: "'If you hold to my teaching, you are really my disciples. Then you will know the truth, and the truth will set you free." (NKJV) The truth is set and built on Jesus (John 1:17) but now, in this day and age, he isn't sitting in front of us to teach us. Instead, what we have is this intimate letter from him, directly to us, in His Holy Bible that will lead us, correct us, and train us for righteousness (2 Timothy 3:16-17), so that we might be equipped to do what we've been called to do. We know and live by His teaching, by reading His Word. And we have His Holy Spirit to help us understand what it means and how it applies to us.

Reading His Word is not just aimlessly skimming through pages looking for a good verse to post on social media. Reading His Word is taking the time to sit down (without distraction) and really study books, chapters, and verses in a search for Jesus, both His character and His instructions, and learn how to apply them to our life. His Words are the keys to a relationship with Him. It may seem challenging at first, and you might perceive it as hard or even drudgery, but...God's word has an amazing ability to come alive! The more we read, the more we want! The more we read, the more it becomes like exquisite tasting food - we can't get enough! And that's when we learn that His word teaches and imparts; the way to live in true freedom as He said in John 8. (How do you think a few thousand-year-old book is still a bestseller?) As we search out these keys and apply them to our lives, they will continually reveal new patterns and thought processes, and give proper direction for life - a life that God designed to be full of freedom.

Let's start with the book of Psalms, which has amazing and encouraging verses:

Psalm 119:11 Your word I have hidden in my heart, that I might not sin against You. (NKJV)

What the author of this psalm provides a powerful description of what the Word does for us! When we can hide (store up or treasure) the Word of God in our hearts (mind, will, and emotions), we will not sin against (hurt, disappoint, miss the mark) the One that we love! The Word allows us to know what would hurt our Father's heart, causing division between us. (1 John 1:9). The psalmist also said in verse 105 that the Word is a "lamp unto my feet, a light unto my path." (NKJV) The Word is what allows us to walk with clarity, without stumbling in the relationship God desires and designed for us.

Psalm 32:8 "I will instruct you and teach you in the way you should go; I will guide you with My eye." (NKJV) King David wrote this powerful psalm and it shows so much of God's heart for us! God wants to instruct us, not to put us in bondage, but to lead us into freedom (remember John 8), and He wants to do it with His eye! Have you ever disappointed someone that you love or respect? The worst part about it is seeing the look on their faces, the look in their eyes that you missed the mark. This is exactly what David was

BUILT

trying to explain to us: when God is leading us, if we are unsure about the next steps, we can look to His Word and then His eye. It will show the way.

Encountering God is his desire for each one of us. Not just a one-time experience; but on a constant and consistent basis. Paul said it like this to the church meeting in the city of Ephesus: "that Christ may dwell in your hearts through faith; that you, being rooted and grounded in love, may be able to comprehend with all the saints what is the width and length and depth and height— to know the love of Christ which passes knowledge; that you may be filled with all the fullness of God." (Ephesians 3:17-19 NKJV) God wants you to *know* His love, not just read about it! It is an encouragement when we read about things or hear about things, but it is a different level when we get to experience something for ourselves! This word "comprehend" is really amazing. Its definition is to "experience," and that is the plan of God's! That we should know the fullness of the love of God by experiencing, thereby having sound knowledge of it.

Question: Do you have a daily Bible reading plan?

_____

_____

_____

The free 30 day "Built" reading plan can be found on Codyrspencer.com

So We Can Know His Promises

2 Peter 1:2 NLT "May God give you more and more grace and peace as you grow in your knowledge of God and Jesus our Lord."

There are a few basic things that we need to know if we are going to be true disciples of Christ.

The first basic thing we need knowledge of is the Bible itself. The Bible is the manual and instruction guide for Christian living. Without it, we would be a mess. This robs us of all that God has for us! When we know the Word we can continue to have victory. When we have knowledge of the Bible, it is not only an idea but it becomes powerful truths we can apply to our hearts. The power of the Bible is even greater than that though! The Bible shows us how to act intelligently so that we can always advance (Joshua 1:7-8). The Bible is so powerful because it is God's truth, available for us to take action upon, and the great thing that we already discussed is, God cannot lie. If He said it, it is the truth and it is available to us!

Here are a few of the promises from Chapter One. Let's visit them for a minute.

Romans 8:37 NKJV "You are more than a conqueror through Christ Jesus."

A conqueror is a champion boxer who trains hard, has great skills, and wins a battle for the belt and the check. But to be more than a conqueror is to be like the champion boxer's wife. She gets to enjoy the victory and all that comes with it without having to go through the battle. The truth is you are not the boxer. You get to be like the wife (sorry guys) and collect the winnings! The Bible declares that you are more than a conqueror through Jesus and what He did on the cross. No longer are you at the mercy of "life" and hardship but you have victory in the name of Jesus!

John 15:1-12 says you have access to full and overflowing joy.

The fact is simple; too many people live in sadness and depression. If we do not know how to break free from it according to the Word, we can never live in it. There is a path to freedom. If we abide in Him (John 15:4), and by doing so we will produce much fruit (John 15:5), in turn keeping His commandments (John 15:10), we will have His joy and our joy will be made full (John 15:12). Jesus did

BUILT

not die for you to endure life; He died that you would have abundant life (John 10:10). Part of that abundance is a joy! Something many people in this world are stripped of.

Colossians 2:10 NKJV says, and you are complete in Him.

So many people have bought lies and feel that they are "not good enough" but that is so far from the truth! When we recognize that in Jesus we are complete, everything changes. It is no longer about our ability, ideas, or even capabilities. The reality is we are now more than enough; our gas tank is "full" and ready to go! Where you felt lacking in your mind, it is now replaced because you have the mind of Christ (1 Corinthians 2:16). Where you thought you were set up to fail because of your personality, it's now in vain because you have all you need in Him! Where you felt that you were not good enough because of your past, Jesus has washed you white as snow! You are complete in Him. Nothing is missing, nothing is broken and nothing is lacking!

Isaiah 41:10 NKJV "'Fear not, for I *am* with you; Be not dismayed, for I *am* your God. I will strengthen you, Yes, I will help you, I will uphold you with My righteous right hand.'"

What an amazing promise from the Lord! Depression and anxiety are problems that run rampant and they are not from God (2 Timothy 1:7). His promise is that we do not need to be afraid because He is with us. He is our God, He will help us and He will uphold us. With those promises, we have NOTHING to fear! How do we access them? Philippians 4:6-7 teaches us that if we pray with supplication (specific and clear) prayer, and with thanksgiving, the peace of God would surpass our understanding. Freedom from fear is a promise from God!

These are a few examples of promises from God found in the Bible. The promises of God are useless unless we know them and the promises we know are useless unless we actively live in them!

Jesus taught and educated His disciples so they could actually live the life that He paid for. How sad would it be as His modern-day disciples to not know His promises that still stand and completely miss out on them? The Bible is not a boring book; it is an unmasking of His desires and promises for His followers. We need to know our Bible so we can have the benefits of Jesus' sacrifice.

Question: What areas are you curious about learning more about? Write them here and create a plan to find them in the Scriptures.

_____

_____

_____

So We Can Know What We are Doing

If we have a million dollars but don't know about it, we can't use it. That's how it is for many people. They desire things but fail to realize those things already in their hands.

We can be taught almost anything; in fact, knowledge is the one thing that lasts and empowers us. If we can only act upon what we know, then we need to know the Word of God. How did Jesus empower, secure, and equip His disciples? By giving them knowledge of His Kingdom. Knowledge is essential for our maturity.

Hosea 4:6 "My people are destroyed for lack of knowledge. Because you have rejected knowledge, I will also reject you from being a priest to Me; because you have forgotten the law of your God, I will also forget your children." (NKJV)

God said it Himself - His people are perishing. Another version says they "are being destroyed" because of a willing lack of knowledge. Too often, people say that they believe what they hear, but upon inspection, it can quickly be concluded that they do not truly know. You need to truly know what you believe so you can stand secure

BUILT

and immovable on that truth. Most people still live life in bondage and lack because they have only heard the truth but they don't know the truth for themselves. It is the Truth (and only the Truth) that makes us free! (John 8:32)

Please don't be a person who only hears something; be a person who knows something. Search out the Scriptures and apply them to your life. They will bring you everything you are currently searching for. We can only serve God to the level of what we know. I want to challenge you to fully know so you can fully serve!

We need to know which areas of our understanding we need to grow so that our spiritual lives will go to new levels. 2 Peter 1:5-9 gives us an amazing rubric or statement of purpose for growth. "In view of all this, make every effort to respond to God's promises. Supplement your faith with a generous provision of moral excellence, and moral excellence with knowledge, and knowledge with self-control, and self-control with patient endurance, and patient endurance with godliness, and godliness with brotherly affection, and brotherly affection with love for everyone. The more you grow like this, the more productive and useful you will be in your knowledge of our Lord Jesus Christ. But those who fail to develop in this way are short-sighted or blind, forgetting that they have been cleansed from their old sins." (NLT) Let's take a closer look at this passage.

Verse nine highlights the "why" that we seek so often! When we grow in this manner, we are keeping ourselves from forgetting the sin we were cleansed from and ensuring we don't get "blind" to His forgiveness. And here is one of the strategies He gave us - supplement your faith with a generous provision of *moral excellence.* One of the first things that the Lord wants us to add to our life after salvation is a lifestyle of good character, The Bible explores good character in so many places, and we have the Holy Spirit to lead and convict us when we fall short (John 16:8). After moral excellence, this passage explains that we need to have a basic *knowledge* of the Word (we will cover what the Bible says is basic). After we have added knowledge, we're to add *self-control*. Self-control is something we will always be working on (refer to chapter 1 of this book), and to know the Word and have a lifestyle of character will help to empower our self-control. To our self-control, add the dreaded (kidding...not kidding) *patient endurance*. Patient endurance is a real challenge to this "on-demand" generation. We can get a ride in a matter of minutes, have our food quickly delivered via an app, stream our favorite shows instantly. These are all good things, but they have taught us the opposite of the value of patience! There is not only value but need, in learning to wait graciously on God's timing, allowing Him to work and remaining in faith all the way through. Then, we want to add to our patient endurance, *godliness*. To godliness, *brotherly affection -* we are really intended to love each other. Many people have a difficult time with this. When we learn to have brotherly affection, it allows us to remain in Him and not in offense and gossip. After brotherly affection, we should add to it *love for everyone*. It is a sign of maturity when we can love everyone, even the seemingly unloveable; to see them through the eyes of Christ no matter who they are or what they've done. To share genuine love towards them by sharing the Gospel with them!

These things are laid out in this manner so that we do not lose sight of who we are in Jesus and what He has done for us. So that we can grow, never returning to the old way of life. Refuse to be a person who passes away because of a lack of knowledge!

Question 1: Have you been growing in the proper way? Describe what that looks like.

BUILT

Question 2: What is one thing you can work on right now to make sure you are growing how God has planned?

_____

_____

_____

So We Can Know Who We Are

Question: Does the toilet paper go over or under while on the roll?

We can argue about it, and it may surprise you to know, but the designer is who determines what way it should go. This is true in our lives as well. The only one who has the right to identify who I am and what I am capable of is God. Why? Because He is the one who designed and created me (Psalm 139:15-16)! We were all designed with purpose and intention from His heart!

P.S. The patent says toilet paper should go over.

There has been a fight for our identity since the very beginning; starting with the fall of man. The enemy is out to steal, to kill, and to destroy, and he knows that if he can take **who** we are - our very identity - he won't even have to worry about plotting to destroy us because, without our identity, we'll do it for him. Let's look at how this goes and how we each can combat it with the Word of God

In the book of Daniel, we find four Jewish boys who had been taken captive by King Nebuchadnezzar, and, according to the tradition of the day, they were to be renamed. Let's check it out in chapter one and verse six and seven, "Now from among those of the sons of Judah were Daniel, Hananiah, Mishael, and Azariah. To them the chief of the eunuchs gave names: he gave Daniel *the name* Belteshazzar; to Hananiah, Shadrach; to Mishael, Meshach; and to Azariah, Abed-Nego." Now, it seems harmless to have their names changed, but it was different back then. Your name was literally what defined you! Look at the table below to see their original names and their new names.

Hananiah = "God has favored"	Shadrach = "royal" or "the great scribe"
Mishael = "who is what God is"	Meshach = "guest of a king"
Azariah = "Jehovah has helped"	Abed-nego = "servant of Nebo"
Daniel = "God is my Judge"	Belteshazzar = "lord of the straitened treasure"

The new name wasn't "bad" but it wasn't what God assigned to them. The truth is the world is *still* trying to give you a name. The other truth is God has given you a name. Most, sadly, never live to learn what God has named them. The difference is what name *you allow* to identify you and who you allow to give it to you! The guy who named these four boys was a priest of the nation that captured them, with a different religion. So often, we encounter a similar situation. Something happens to us and we are labeled by the world. We should not allow that label to stick; it's not from God. People will run with those names and labels for their entire lives, making life decisions from this label someone assigned to them because they bought the lie of that false name. How we are defined should not be from an outside opinion, but rather, the source of our name should only be from the Word of God.

Daniel refused to allow the name assigned him by the world to determine who he was and the actions took. We find in Daniel chapter one verse eight, "But Daniel purposed in his heart that he would not defile himself with the portion of the king's delicacies, nor with the wine which he drank; therefore he requested of the chief of

BUILT

the eunuchs that he might not defile himself." Our identity will form our realities! According to Proverbs 23 verse seven, it says, "For as he thinks in his heart, so *is* he." (NKJV) Daniel knew who He was despite His situation and problems, and despite what others were saying about Him. When you know the Word of God you'll know what it says about who you are! The moment we start to live in that identity is the moment our real success can begin!

If you believe you can't (do something, be something, live something), then you are absolutely correct. And that's why the devil will try so hard to make you believe it! This tactic of the devils is demonstrated throughout the Word of God and in some mighty people's lives. What you believe about yourself in your heart is how you will live. If you know who you are, you will not allow yourself to be anything except vigilant to protect your name... Instead, you will chase hard the purpose God has for your life. If we fail to educate ourselves we will believe falsely about ourselves in our hearts, and that, in turn, can cause us to create realities that do not help us achieve God's plans for our life.

Question 1: List the first three words you define yourself with?

_____

_____

_____

Question 2: Where did they come from? From God or from experiences and people?

_____

_____

_____

Question 3: If it was not from God, what can you do to change the way you think of and label yourself.?

_____

_____

_____

So We Can Stand Strong

According to the Guinness World Book of Records, "The tallest free-standing house of cards measured 25 feet 9 7/16 inches and was built by Bryan Berg on 16 October 2007." If you look at the images online, this card house is mind-blowing! It is tall (obviously) but the builder also added some extra designs and layers. It must have taken him years of practice in order to get that right. What's crazy about the whole card house is that one slight, small breeze could destroy everything he was building. Sadly, many "disciples" are like card houses. Because they are not built on a strong foundation, they can be easily blown over or around when challenges arise. I would not have this be your story. They have a long-standing history in the church but the moment something happens they can be blown over. Jesus talked about this in Matthew 7:26-27, "'But everyone who hears these sayings of Mine, and does not do them, will be like a foolish man who built his house on the sand: and the rain descended, the floods came, and the winds blew and beat on that house, and it fell. And great was its fall.'" (NKJV) We as disciples need to know the Word so we are not like a card house. We don't want to be like the house built on sand. We want to stand under any circumstances!

Here is what the Word says about itself:

- It is like milk (to help nurture and grow up) Hebrews 5:12-14
- It is solid food (for those who are mature) 1 Corinthians 3:1-2
- It is a sword (to expose the heart and truth) Hebrews 4:12
- It is like fire and a hammer (to burn up and remodel) Jeremiah 23:29
- It is like a mirror (to self reflect and measure ourselves) James 1:23-25
- It is a lamp and a light (to show the right direction and steps) Psalm 119:105

BUILT

- It is like water (to bring cleansing) Ephesians 5:26
- It is like gold (how desirable it is) and sweeter than honey (Psalm 19:10)
- It is like an anchor (to keep us secure) Hebrews 6:18-19

With all of this, we can stand strong in any situation.

We have an enemy in this world, and his goals and desires are to completely destroy us. John 10:10 says it like this: "The thief does not come except to steal, and to kill, and to destroy." (NKJV) We need to know the Word because that is what we use, live by and "fight" with. It's not about creative ideas and plans to go against spiritual attacks (Ephesians 6:12). It is the Word of God from a position of faith. These attacks are normal, they should be expected and they mean that you are doing something of worth for the Kingdom. Why would an enemy attack if you are feeding into his plans? Sometimes the enemy will use situations, other times he will use people, but often it will be a lie he sneaks into your heart. 1 Peter 3 verse 15 tells us to "*be* ready to *give* a defense to everyone who asks you a reason for the hope that is in you, with meekness and fear." (NKJV) We want to be able to stand strong against any temptation or attack that is thrown your way!

Jesus Himself experienced this in Matthew chapter four, starting in verse 1: "Then Jesus was led by the Spirit into the wilderness to be tempted there by the devil. For forty days and forty nights he fasted and became very hungry. During that time the devil came and said to him, 'If you are the Son of God, tell these stones to become loaves of bread.' But Jesus told him, 'No! The Scriptures say, 'People do not live by bread alone, but by every word that comes from the mouth of God.' Then the devil took him to the holy city, Jerusalem, to the highest point of the Temple, and said, 'If you are the Son of God, jump off! For the Scriptures say, "He will order his angels to protect you. And they will hold you up with their hands so you won't even hurt your foot on a stone."' Jesus responded, 'The Scriptures also say, "You must not test the Lord your God."' Next the devil took him to the peak of a very high mountain and showed him all the kingdoms of the world and their glory. 'I will give it all to you,' he said, 'if you will kneel down and worship me.' 'Get out of here, Satan,' Jesus told him. 'For the Scriptures say, "You must worship the Lord your God and serve only him."' Then the devil went away, and angels came and took care of Jesus." (NKJV)

What we see here is the enemy attacking Jesus' identity and natural, human, desires. What Jesus used to fend off the attack is what we should use - the Word! Jesus was hungry, and he surely wanted to eat bread and be nourished after 40 days, but He recognized this for what it was: an attack, a test. He could have thrown Himself off the Temple and the angels would have protected Him, but he knew it was an attack; a test. He could have bowed down and accepted that temporary authority, but He knew it was an attack; a test. The last temptation, to get the Son of God to kneel down and worship him, was the enemy's primary goal. It is important to know the Word so we do not fall into the traps the enemy will set. The only real power he has, in truth, is to lie and attempt to trick us. When we know the Word, we can test the intentions, as Jesus did, to assure we can stand strong in the face of the enemy's lies.

These attacks are sneaky and come in the form of lies, manipulation, and intimidation. When we know who we are and what the Word says, we will not fall into those traps. 1 Peter 5:8 teaches us that we need to be "sober and vigilant" because we have an enemy "seeking whom he may devour." Don't be scared; he is a toothless lion and has a good roar, but that's it. To be sober and vigilant is to stay alert. know the truth, and hold on to it tightly. That way, when he comes, he gets sent packing quickly.

Question 1: What lies has the enemy been trying to use on you?

_____

_____

_____

Question 2: What does the Word say about those lies?

_____

_____

_____

Question 3: Write a rebuke with the Word to have it ready when you next identify an attack.

_____

_____

_____

The Word Exposes Our Hearts

Have you ever gotten ready for the day and but not looked into the mirror until you were already at school or work? It can be a heart-sinking moment when you realize there is a giant toothpaste stain in the middle of your shirt or even worse, what you thought was black is blue and you now look like you got dressed in the dark? Lighting and mirrors are valuable tools when getting ready for the day.

Just as a mirror helps us to see our outside, the Bible is the tool for checking the position of our hearts. The writer of Hebrews reveals this truth to us in chapter 4 verse 12: "For the word of God *is* living and powerful, and sharper than any two-edged sword, piercing even to the division of soul and spirit, and of joints and marrow, and is a discerner of the thoughts and intents of the heart." (NKJV) When we come to know and love the Word of God, it's easy to agree that it's one of the most powerful tools in the world. It can be so easy to fool ourselves and others that our hearts are in the right place, but the Bible will reveal the truth and it exposes every single part of the heart, thoughts, and intentions. In Proverbs 27:19, it says, "As in water face *reflects* face, so a man's heart *reveals* the man." (NKJV) The Bible shows us the reflection of our true selves, our hearts.

The truth is our thoughts form our actions, and when our thoughts are corrected, our actions will follow! When we allow Philippians 4:8 to govern our thought life, and think on these things: whatever things are true, whatever things are noble, whatever things are just, whatever things are pure, whatever things are lovely, whatever things are of good report, if there is any virtue and if there is anything praiseworthy—meditate on these things. We often find it easy to dwell on negative thoughts, failures, faults, and sins. But you can count on the Bible to point out not only our problems (conviction) but what to focus and meditate on so that we can move toward and then remain in a place of purity!

Intentions are a funny thing. Have you ever noticed that we judge other people on their actions, but we judge ourselves based on our intentions? We can get angry or annoyed at people who believe they are trying to do something good, but the results are not what they intended. But, (oh, my) when we make a mistake, we try to explain it over with our good intentions to justify our missteps. The Lord knows our intentions. The Bible reveals our true intentions, which can be scary, to help bring us into a place of right standing with God. It does this by showing us where we truly are versus, where we think we are, and then, it shows the path to close that distance!

The Bible is a gift from God to expose our hearts - whether good or bad - to bring us into the right position with Him. Many people avoid the Bible because it demands change. We want to stay self-justified in our "good intentions" because "God knows my heart." Ah, but yes! He really does know our hearts and He gave us the Bible to reveal our hearts to ourselves. Not only does He not want us to live in ignorance about what we believe, He wants us to live in greater and greater knowledge of ourselves. The Bible gives us the truth and direction to truly have God's intentions and know we have God's heart in us (Ezekiel 36:26).

BUILT

Question 1: What things are competing for your heart today?

_____

_____

_____

Question 2: Are you aware of things you are hiding from that God would like to work with you on? Are you afraid to work on this with God? What do you think the end result would be?

_____

_____

_____

Take time to pray and study the Word every day, starting today. You might be in the best place you have ever been; you might find something small or there might be a glaring problem that needs to be aligned. No matter what it is, God never exposes it to hurt us, only to better our relationship. And He is a gentle counselor, you do not need to be afraid or worry.

What's next? It's wonderful that, as disciples of Jesus, we have everything we need to "grow" and do this according to His plans. This step in discipleship is not one we move on from; it is one that we build upon over time. Life as a disciple is never boring! In reality, we are only as strong as what we know. I challenge you to continue learning and applying the Word of God to your life every day and in every situation. Allow Him to build you - your faith, your love, your life.

Cody Spencer

FOUNDATION FOUR

EMPOWERED

* * *

Matthew 10:1-8 "Jesus called his twelve disciples to him and gave them authority to drive out impure spirits and to heal every disease and sickness. These twelve Jesus sent out with the following instructions: 'Do not go among the Gentiles or enter any town of the Samaritans. Go rather to the lost sheep of Israel. As you go, proclaim this message: The kingdom of heaven has come near.' Heal the sick, raise the dead, cleanse those who have leprosy, drive out demons. Freely you have received; freely give." (NKJV)

Jesus taught and revealed who He was to His disciples after He had gained their trust, He did something that seems so scary to so many of us: He *empowered* them. Jesus put power into His people! You have power when you are living with purpose. You gain a position of power through victory of all the things you went through to get here, to such a time as this, and you are not alone in this mission. We just have to get off of the sidelines and use what God has placed in us!

BUILT

We Have Authority

As empowered Christians, we need to recognize that we have authority. We are not weak people who run around in the hope of doing great things for God. We have great power from heaven and we need to exercise it.

John 14:10-14 "'Do you not believe that I am in the Father and the Father in Me? The words that I speak to you I do not speak on My own authority, but the Father who dwells in Me does the works. Believe Me that I am in the Father and the Father in Me, or else believe Me for the sake of the works themselves. Most assuredly I say to you, he who believes in Me, the works that I do he will do also; and greater works than these he will do because I go to My Father. And whatever you ask in My name, that I will do, that the Father may be glorified in the Son. If you ask anything in My name, I will do it.'" (NKJV)

Jesus is here for you, praying for you! He says that we will do even greater works than He did. And now we know that those works require power and authority. God did not send us on a mission all alone. Look at those He sent out in Luke chapter 10 verses 17 through 20: "Then the seventy returned with joy, saying, 'Lord, even the demons are subject to us in Your name.' And He said to them, 'I saw Satan fall like lightning from heaven. Behold, I give you authority to trample on serpents on scorpions, and over all the power of the enemy and nothing shall by any means hurt you. Nevertheless do not rejoice in this, that the spirits are subject to you, but rather rejoice because your names are written in heaven.'" (NKJV) We can see that they were given authority over the things that would try to stop them on their mission, even before Jesus conquered the grave. Imagine now how much you have been empowered following the resurrection of Jesus and the gift of the Holy Spirit! The life of a disciple is not feeble and defeated; it is equipped with authority and power from heaven. You have been given the right tools for the job! Say this out loud: "I am not weak; I am strong in Jesus."

Question 1: In what ways do you demonstrate that you are strong and have authority? What ways are lacking?

_____

_____

_____

Question 2: Do you think that others detect that your life has authority? If not, how can you start to have that shift today?

_____

_____

_____

With Power

If you had been hired to cut down 12 trees and had the option to use an ax or a chainsaw, you would pick the chainsaw. It would save time, effort, and energy. The same is true for the life of a disciple. He has sent us the Holy Spirit to equip us with the power to fulfill our purpose and His plans.

This is not about what we can do on our own. This is about being given and then utilizing our supernatural backing and support. People who don't understand this gift of supernatural support may have different opinions, but it is an amazing gift from God to enable us to accomplish what we've been purposed to do. No one in this life will fully accomplish what God has for them without His power working in them. You have access to power in this life. It is not a "single-player mission" because you now have the Spirit of God in you (Romans 8:11).

Jesus' disciples were told to go and wait for this promise before anything else because it was so important. In Acts chapter one verse eight, Jesus told them what the promise would produce in

BUILT

their lives: "'You will receive power to bear witness of Me.'" (NKJV) This promise is to equip you with every tool (power) you will need to be a witness to others. The Holy Spirit will equip you with boldness (Acts 4:29), the words to say, and even where to say them. This changes everything! Those who are "introverts" now have the boldness to speak to others; those who live in fear of what to say can hear directly from Holy Spirit. Every natural obstacle that would have been in the way has been removed by the Holy Spirit!

In 1 Corinthians 2:4, Paul was writing to the church in Corinth, and he told them: "'And my speech and my preaching *were* not with persuasive words of human wisdom, but in demonstration of the Spirit and of power, that your faith should not be in the wisdom of men but in the power of God.'" (NKJV) Paul understood that he had power from the Holy Spirit, and that, in order to help establish people's hearts in Jesus, they needed more than his words to believe him, they also needed a demonstration of what he was talking about. The instructions are given in Mark 16:15-18, that disciples have the commission to go and preach the good news to all creatures and, yes, even today, signs will follow them. These signs followed Paul and should follow you as well. The signs are that you will cast out demons (yes, it's a real thing even today), speak in new tongues (refer back to the end of Chapter 1 of this book), take up serpents, drink deadly things (for clarity it is not telling you to drink poison and play with deadly snakes, but that if you are fulfilling the call of God you will have His hand of protection. See Acts 28:1-10 for an example), and that you will lay hands on the sick, and they will recover! These are things that Paul and the other disciples experienced in their lives. The truth is, as a follower and disciple of Jesus, these things can be active in your life as well!

The Holy Spirit works in and through believers to give them power and authority. Just like Jesus said, greater works YOU shall do!

Question 1: Do these signs follow you? Name a time when you think they did.

_____

_____

Question 2: Are you ready for God to use you in this way? Do you have fear? Are you willing anyway?

_____

_____

The start is being willing and having the desire. Say this with me right now: "I am available and will be used by God today." Now your job is to prepare yourself.

For more teaching on this, I would suggest the following:

Surprised by the Spirit: Jack Deere
The Believers Authority: Kenneth Hagin

In Victory

Romans 16:20, "The God of peace will soon crush Satan under your feet. The grace of our Lord Jesus be with you." (NKJV) You are not fighting an uphill battle, a strong opponent, or even an opponent with great power. You are fighting from a place of victory, which Jesus won on the cross. When we understand the place we are fighting from, we can truly operate in a greater level of authority!

Ephesians chapter 1 verses 18 through 21 teaches us this: "the eyes of your understanding being enlightened; that you may know what is the hope of His calling, what are the riches of the glory of His inheritance in the saints, and what *is* the exceeding greatness of His power toward us who believe, according to the working of His mighty power which He worked in Christ when He raised Him from

BUILT

the dead and seated *Him* at His right hand in the heavenly *places,* far above all principality and power and might and dominion, and every name that is named, not only in this age but also in that which is to come." (NKJV)

This is from one of the Apostle Paul's prayers for a church he was teaching; the church of Ephesus. Let's talk about that section of Scripture and what we can learn about our position. His first point in this prayer is that "the eyes of their understanding be enlightened". He is praying the Holy Spirit will enable them to fully see what he was about to say to them, and not filter it from their own point of view or past experiences... We want to approach this in the same way, so take a moment and pray, asking God to help you see what is about to be said. Here, Paul lays out the truth, that there is exceeding greatness of His power toward us who believe. Not a little bit of power. An exceeding greatness of power! This power is both for us and will be through us to impact the world, that we may overcome and show others the same truth. And where did this power come from? It came from the same mighty power that raised Christ from the grave, brought Him back to heaven, and placed Him next to God, above all things in this world, both now and anything that is to come. This is called power. This is called victory. And it's available to work in you and through you!

Paul also taught the Christians in the city of Rome (Romans 8:11) that "if the Spirit of Him who raised Jesus from the dead dwells in you, He who raised Christ from the dead will also give life to your mortal bodies through His Spirit who dwells in you." (NKJV) So, we are not fighting for *the* victory, but we are fighting *from a position* of victory (having already won the war!) When we are living out the call and purpose of God in our lives, when we fully see and understand what Paul was teaching in Ephesians 1, not only will we have a real-life here on earth plus eternal life, but we will also have access to that exceeding power!

Question: Where have you been "fighting" from; as though you are in second place (or worse?) or from the position of victory? What changes can you make to have a different approach?

In Our Purpose

While in a business class in college, I was assigned a final project. About one month before the end of class, we were placed into teams of four. I looked around at my classmates with high hopes, I knew that by working together, we could create an amazing final project. My teammates were smart and even had some experience in business. We formulated a master plan with our individual assignments and set off to get our work done. But. Have you ever been on a group project at school or work? You may have experienced what II learned from that project (and not much of it was about business). That month I learned that many group projects turn into one person working extremely hard to finish a final project, feeling very much alone. But God is not like people (Num. 23:19)! The great thing with God is, even though it may feel like you are alone in His work, you are not. You have the Spirit of God with you on every mission! And not just with you, but empowering you to accomplish what He has asked you to do!

Acts 1:8: "'But you shall receive power when the Holy Spirit has come upon you, and you shall be witnesses to Me in Jerusalem, and in all Judea and Samaria, and to the end of the earth.'" (NKJV)

The purpose of the empowerment of God is two-fold: First, it's to bring freedom to your life, and, second, to help you bring freedom to others' lives. Just before this amazing encounter with the Holy Spirit, Peter (Remember Peter? The disciple who denied Jesus and then went back to fishing?) could be described as someone who was not "bold" and was running from God's expectations for his life. Something amazing happened to him after this experience in Acts with the Holy Spirit. The crowds started to mock what God was doing (Acts 2:13) and Peter, now being filled and at work on his commission, stood up in front of 3,000 men and boldly responded to their false accusations, leading them to believe in the message of Jesus and salvation (Acts 2:14-39). When we are living in our purpose and working in the purpose and authority we have from heaven, we are powerful! You have access to that same power!

We must commit to....
Doing the work.
Depending on God's power and not our own.
Doing what He asks no matter how awkward or "scary" it may seem.

Question 1: Do you feel like you are losing in a battle? Have you asked God for help? Have you asked God if this is even a fight that you should be involved in?

_____

_____

_____

Question 2: Are you living in your purpose? How do you know this? How is it demonstrated in your life?

_____

_____

_____

If so, you need to remind yourself today that you can only have victory if you are in obedience to God.

Not Hearers Only

James 1:22 "But be doers of the word, and not hearers only, deceiving yourselves." (NKJV)

Many Christians who have so much knowledge of the Word but very little application of it. We can all agree that knowledge is necessary, but what good is it if we never put it into action? God gave us His Word to empower us to live it out, not just to hear it out! True success and progress happen when we live out the Word. As believers, we need to engage the promises of God!

It's the same as any relationship. If the other party involved constantly tells you their thoughts, feelings, and expectations but you never follow through on them, can we actually expect to have progress? As we live out this relationship with God, we need to truly understand that the Word is here to empower us to do what God has asked us to do. The key to actually *having* what the Word talks about is *doing* what the Word talks about.

If you are unsure about what to do for God, here are a few starting points from the Word that each and every single believer is called to do.
- Share Jesus with others (Mark 16:15).
- Disciple them (Matthew 28:19).
- Cast out demons (Mark 16:17).
- Speak in new tongues (Mark 16:17).
- Lay hands on the sick (Mark 16:18).
- Love your neighbor as yourself (Mark 12:31).

When we start to do the things God asks us to do, our relationship with God grows. When we ignore these requests and commands of God, our relationship tends to grow dull. In order to be empowered, we must take steps of action! Commit today to take steps of action.

Question 1: What action step will you take today to not being a hearer only?

_____
_____
_____

Question 2: If you couldn't fail at any of these what one would you do most*?

_____
_____
_____

BUILT

Perfect, you can't fail, so do it every day this week!

The truth is that Jesus does not only desire disciples to be people who know Him personally and have a knowledge of Him, but also to do the work that He has given them! Too many people have asked the question, "What now?" or "What about me?", thinking that God has no intention of using them. You are empowered by the spirit of God to do the work of God! This life is not one where we are simply placed on the sidelines with the knowledge of what to do; it comes with the empowerment to "get out onto the field" and do it as well. Many people sit on the sidelines t because they think God's work is only for pastors and their staff members. This is the opposite of the truth! When you decide to not just be a hearer but to live in your purpose and with the power of God, then you step into the reality of being a true disciple!

Cody Spencer

FOUNDATION FIVE

COMMISSIONED

* * *

When convicted thief and murderer Charles Peace was being escorted to the gallows, he was accompanied by a clergyman reading from *The Consolations of Religion* about the "flames never quenched." Peace was a known criminal for whom the public had no sympathy. No one can say with confidence the prison chaplain was reading without a sneer. Nevertheless, some of the last words this man heard on earth detailed the waiting wrath for unrepentant traitors of the Most High. Incredulous, Peace turned to the chaplain and exclaimed, "Sir, if I believed what you and the church of God say that you believe, even if England were covered with broken glass from coast to coast, I would walk over it, if need be, on hands and knees and think it worthwhile living, just to save one soul from an eternal hell like that!"

Too many people, when asked why they don't share the Gospel, say they don't have enough time, they are scared, they don't want to get hurt, etc. The reality is, it is not a suggestion; it is a commandment! When Jesus came to His disciples, he gave them an opportunity. He said, "Follow Me and I will make you fishers of men." And when He left them, He asked, no, commanded something that would change the direction of the world: "Go and create disciples of the whole world, teaching them all I have taught you." When we answer the call to receive Jesus, we are committing to the Great Commission. Living out the Great Commission is a part of filling the Greatest Commandment - love God with all that you have and love others as yourself. Jesus' idea of a disciple is someone who wins, disciples, and teaches others to do the same. Without this, each generation of believers would die, leaving no one to spread the news to those who have not heard and who are coming in the future.

Many people don't share the Gospel because they are focused on other things, things of this world. They may be good things, but we must remember that we're servants of God before we're anything else. Are you a plumber or a servant of the Most High God? We don't demonstrate with our words; we demonstrate it based on how we spend our time. Here is a way to look at this to help determine the importance of what we do with our time: If it doesn't have eternal value, it's worthless. The Bible says it this way: "While we do not look at the things which are seen, but at the things which are not seen; for the things which are seen are temporal, but the things which are not seen are eternal." (2 Corinthians 4:18 NKJV)

Too many people don't witness because they feel like they are just "aren't ready." But really, the best way to get ready is to just *do it*. No one "feels ready" for a child, but most parents quickly learn it's a part of our nature to know what to do and when to do it. You can read all the parenting books in the world, but until you actually have a child, you don't know what you can do! It's the same with your spiritual nature. Discipleship is best learned with on-the-job-training. This is also the season in which you will grow in your relationship rapidly.

When we don't disciple others, it shows that Lordship is not established in our hearts. If Jesus is Lord, we follow His expectations beyond our comfort or excuses. We must live a life of refusing to negotiate with what God has called us to do; a life of no procrastination and without hesitation. In Luke chapter 9, we find three different people trying to present Jesus with these excuses. Let us check them out in verses 57-62.

Luke 9:57 "As they were walking along, someone said to Jesus, 'I will follow you wherever you go.' But Jesus replied, 'Foxes have dens to live in, and birds have nests, but the Son of Man has no place even to lay his head.' He said to another person, 'Come, follow me.' The man agreed, but he said, 'Lord, first let me return home and bury my father.' But Jesus told him, 'Let the spiritually dead bury their own dead! Your duty is to go and preach about the Kingdom of God.' Another said, 'Yes, Lord, I will follow you, but first let me say good-bye to my family.' But Jesus told him, 'Anyone who puts a hand to the plow and then looks back is not fit for the Kingdom of God.'" (NLT)

Why do we need a life of creating disciples? Why should we fulfill the Great Commission? Why do we need to live without negotiating this call? Why do we need to throw off procrastination and hesitation? Because Heaven and Hell are real and their reality is a driving force. I pray that this verse from the book of Isaiah chapter 5 and verse 14 will shake your heart: "Therefore Sheol has enlarged itself and opened its mouth beyond measure." (NKJV) Yes, Sheol (Hell) had to open its mouth wider for those whom it would consume. Can you be a person who sets a personal goal to shut the mouth of hell and create disciples in a way that heaven has to be made larger?

Question 1: Will you commit to creating disciples as a part of your lifestyle?

_____
_____
_____

Question 2: What do you think will get in the way of this decision most?

_____
_____
_____

The Great Commission

Before Jesus left his disciples on the earth, He gave them one main instruction. We find this in Matthew 28 verses 18 through 20. It's important to remember that Jesus had been "discipling" His followers for over 3 years. While this might have been one of the last things He said to them, it is also the final piece of direction for them as His followers. Let's look at them together to see what Jesus was telling them.

Matthew 28:18: "And Jesus came and spoke to them, saying, 'All authority has been given to Me in heaven and on earth. Go therefore and make disciples of all the nations, baptizing them in the name of the Father and of the Son and of the Holy Spirit, teaching them to observe all things that I have commanded you; and lo, I am with you always, *even* to the end of the age.' Amen." (NKJV)

All Authority

Imagine getting the keys to your dream car and you are given these simple instructions: "Do what you want but when you come back, bring one more person with you." Uh, yeah! Deal! And the next thing you know, you are cruising down the highway, stopping where everyone can see you driving the car, and then returning that night with no one else in it with you. Sure, it was fun while it lasted, but do you think you would ever be able to drive it again? Do you think the one who gave you the authority to do and go where you wanted would be happy with how you failed to do the one thing they had asked?

Jesus' death was the payment for our sins but his resurrection was for authority to be returned to its rightful place. The Bible teaches us that, when Jesus died, it was for the sins of the world (John 1:29) and that the only payment accepted for sin was the shedding of blood (Hebrews 9:22). By His death on the cross, the payment for sins was completed. But there was more. Our Savior is not still in a grave, he defeated the grave! Not only did He defeat the grave, but He also defeated the enemy by taking back the keys of sin, death, and the grave (Revelation 1:18)!

With this authority, Jesus now declares that He is passing it on to us, but with this authority, there is purpose. He said, "All authority has been given to me in heaven and on earth. GO…" The purpose of receiving authority is to go and fulfill what He has called you to do, knowing that, whatever God has called us to do, we've been given the tools to accomplish it.

Go, Therefore

This is a call for every person who professes to be a believer in Jesus Christ. It is easy to find a way to discount yourself or make excuses as to why you cannot do it. The reality is, it's not just for pastors, elders, perfect people, or mature Christians; this is a call for each and every one of us. We must stop sitting in our chairs so long that they become a perfect mold of our bodies. We must stop hiding in our buildings. We must answer the call to go!

To "go" should be one of the most pressing thoughts in our minds every single day. If we don't go, who will? Here's a hard pill to swallow - no-one else is coming. *We* are God's plan to go and tell others. There is no other plan aside from us preaching the Good News about Jesus to those who need to hear it. Check out what Romans 10 says about it in verse 14: "How then shall they call on Him in whom they have not believed? And how shall they believe in Him of whom they have not heard? And how shall they hear without a preacher?" (NKJV) If we are going to call ourselves disciples of Jesus, we must make the commitment to go. No matter the cost, no matter how it makes us feel. No matter the rejection. No matter if the whole world is against us. Go.

And Teach

In the same way, someone is (or should be) walking with you, that's what you need to do for others. In Proverbs 11:30 it states, "…And he who wins souls *is* wise." (NKJV) I want to be wise in the eyes of God. Winning a soul is more than someone saying a prayer with you. It is not even getting them to show up to a class or go to church. The word *teach* means we're to enroll people into a new lifestyle. The same way Jesus did in Matthew 4:19 with the call to His disciples to "follow Me." What we are called to do is enroll others into the same lifestyle we have; one that follows Jesus as our Lord frees us from bondage renews our minds, knows our purpose, grows in our knowledge of Jesus, empowers us, and lastly, that creates more disciples.

This is not a small thing we are enrolling people to do. It is not a small thing that we have done, but it is God's plan and intention. Luke 9 and verse 23 and 24 describes perfectly what we are enrolling people into: "Then He said to *them* all, 'If anyone desires to come after Me, let him deny himself, and take up his cross daily, and follow Me. For whoever desires to save his life will lose it, but whoever loses his life for My sake will save it.'" (NKJV) Enlisting someone in a life of following Jesus, denying themselves, and representing the cross every single day, no matter what is no small thing. You are calling people to find their life by losing it inside of Jesus! This is what we were made for: To be followers of Jesus and to create help as many as possible find themselves in Him.

All Nations

The Great Commission has no room for racism, sexism, nationalism, distance, cliques, social class, economic brackets, style of clothing, or preference. Every single person that has breath in their lungs is eternal and we are called to create disciples of them. If we only desire to fulfill the Great Commandment (loving God) and not the Great Commission, we fall short. I believe it is impossible to love God and not love the people He has created. And, for the record, "all nations" also includes your own state, region, county, and city. Oftentimes people feel led to go overseas, and of course, I support that 100%, but I also believe your city needs Jesus and while you are there, it is your commission. Begin where you are planted.

"Baptizing them in the name of the Father and the Son and the Holy Spirit. Teach these new disciples to obey all the commands I have given you."

I think we've established this: We are to teach others what Jesus taught the disciples, in its entirety; not just what we like or feel comfortable with. We will learn these things by reading His instructions, being disciples ourselves, and then passing them on with clarity. And then...where to start? Start by introducing Lordship into their life just like this book did, building on each chapter like this book did for you. Add in what you are learning, giving thought to their own current circumstances, and what they may personally need. Share your testimony with people and then the Good News of the cross and resurrection of Jesus. What are some practical steps to this?

- For those who surrender their lives to Jesus, start teaching them from the Bible and from this book.
- Get them involved in a church! What do I mean by that? Help them attend regularly, even if you have to pick them up at first. Serving in the church in some capacity.
- Walk with them through this book, walk with them in their relationship with God, and stay with it.
- Challenge them to "go, therefore" as well, and do with and for someone else what you have done with them.

Then? You "go, therefore" into all of the world, creating disciples for Jesus! You cannot imagine where this service to the Lord might take you!

And lo I am with you always, even to the end of the age, Amen!

You are not alone in this, you have the "I Am" with you always! The same "I Am" that was in the burning bush, the same "I Am" that declared it in the garden while being taken captive (John 16:8) promised to be with you along this journey of fulfilling the Great Commandment! Not just from time to time, but until the end of the age! When you feel discouraged, He is there. When you feel weak in your mission, He is there. When you may be rejected, He is there. When someone starts this journey with you, He is there. In every single instance of creating disciples, He is there. The promise is that while we are on this mission, we are never alone!

Write 10 names today
1.   6.
2.   7.
3.   8.
4.   9.
5.   10.

We Need an Urgency

"We'll have all eternity to celebrate our victories, but only one short hour before sunset to win them". - Robert Moffat

Regret is one of the worst emotions you can encounter in this life. Regret is something that cannot be undone. Especially when it is because of something that was left undone. Then, it's a missed moment that may echo through eternity. Those missed moments do not have to exist in your life. When it comes to spreading the Good News, the best way to avoid regret is to live with a sense of urgency and obedience in sharing Jesus every single day.

If you knew that Jesus was coming tomorrow, I am confident that you would not sit back and "hope" someone else finds out how to avoid an eternity in Hell. I can see it now; folks calling everyone that they can, going to the closest grocery store and shouting it over the intercom, pulling into the news station to beg to get a spot on the live broadcast for the night. Urgency makes people do uncommon things. The sad part and the hard truth is, we do not know when Jesus is returning, but we often live as it will be after our lifetime. We act as if we have an eternity of opportunities to share Jesus, but we don't know when someone might slip into that eternity, lost forever! We must make a commitment to live with an urgency to create disciples because eternity is "only a short hour" in front of us.

Question 1: Do you live with an urgency to share Jesus and create disciples? If not, do you know why?

_____

_____

_____

Question 2: Since you now know how important it is, how can you develop such an urgency?

_____

_____

_____

Question 3: I know that everyone is different. Your sense of urgency will look different on you. What do you think it looks like?

_____

_____

_____

My Personal Challenge to You

Master and build on these steps and fulfill the Great Commandment and Commission! Love God with all of your heart, soul, mind, and strength and love your neighbor as yourself. Truly submit your life

BUILT

to Jesus in Lordship and you will find that He is everything you were searching for in the world and everything that you will need in this life. By living with Him as Lord, you will have everything else opened up to you by Him (Matthew 6:33). Refuse to sit on the throne of your heart another day, and choose to live with him as the only "Jehovah" in your life.

Take the time, now, to find what Jesus called you to do and then do it. No matter how far along in life you are, or if you haven't even started looking for a career, do what Jesus asked you to do. It's not about money or recognition. Both of those may come, but what you will certainly have is success and satisfaction knowing that you completed what your Lord asked you to do. One of my personal goals is to be able to say what Jesus said in John 17:4 "'I have glorified You on the earth. I have finished the work which You have given Me to do'" (NKJV) when I get to heaven. Will it actually happen? I am working at it and pray you will as well!

Learn the things of God and the Word of God. Joshua 1:8 "'This Book of the Law shall not depart from your mouth, but you shall meditate in it day and night, that you may observe to do according to all that is written in it. For then you will make your way prosperous, and then you will have good success.'" (NKJV) God wants you to be successful and His plan is found in His Word. Be a student of the Bible for the rest of your life.

Do the things of God. We have an epidemic of Christians who rarely take action. Please do not be a Christian who only consumes. Do the work of God, do not be hearers only (James 1:22), and watch all that God does through your hands in this world. I believe it will be said about this generation: "These are the ones who turned the world upside down." (Acts 17:6b NKJV)

Build these things in others. In other words, disciple someone - everyone that you can! It is the purpose of God for your life and the plan of God for the kingdom to increase. Find one person to start with and help establish these steps and principles into their heart. And by doing so, fulfill the Great Commission.

We may never graduate from these steps, but we can grow in them daily.

This is about fulfilling the Great Commandment and the Great Commission. This is about knowing Him and making Him known! This is what it means to be built by our Lord and Savior, the Master Craftsman.

About the Author

Cody Spencer has been in ministry at His Tabernacle Family Church in Horseheads, NY for the last ten years. He has a Bachelor's Degree in Christian Leadership.

Cody is currently serving as the Youth Pastor of His Tabernacle Family Church. When it comes to working with teens, he always takes a hands-on approach, discipling his students and guiding them through the many challenges they face.

Built was written as a foundational guide for living a successful, prosperous and abundant life as a believer. It is designed to be a helpful discipling tool to accompany believers as they strive to reach the next level in their walks with God.

Cody is married to his beautiful wife, Mindy, and they have two children.

www.codyrspencer.com

Copyright Page

Scripture quotations marked (NLT) are taken from the Holy Bible, New Living Translation, copyright © 1996, 2004, 2007, 2013, 2015 by Tyndale House Foundation. Used by permission of Tyndale House Publishers, Inc., Carol Stream, Illinois 60188. All rights reserved.

"Scripture taken from the New King James Version. Copyright © 1982 by Thomas Nelson, Inc. Used by permission. All rights reserved."

"Scripture quotations taken from the Amplified® Bible (AMP), Copyright © 2015 by The Lockman Foundation Used by permission. www.Lockman.org"

http://www.guinnessworldrecords.com/world-records/tallest-house-of-cards

All words studies taken from "blueletterbible.com"

Made in the USA
Monee, IL
18 January 2022